GW00862699

just
**THE
JOB**

*Care &
Community*

just
**THE
JOB**

Care &
Community

Lifetime Careers
WILTSHIRE

Hodder & Stoughton
A MEMBER OF THE HODDER HEADLINE GROUP

Just the Job! draws directly on the CLIPS careers information database developed and maintained by Lifetime Careers Wiltshire and used by almost every careers service in the UK. The database is revised annually using a rigorous update schedule and incorporates material collated through desk/telephone research and information provided by all the professional bodies, institutions and training bodies with responsibility for course accreditation and promotion of each career area.

ISBN 0 340 68793 2
First published 1997

Impression number   10 9 8 7 6 5 4 3 2 1
Year   2002 2001 2000 1999 1998 1997

Printed in Great Britain for Hodder & Stoughton Educational, the educational publishing division of Hodder Headline Plc, 338 Euston Road, London NW1 3BH, by Cox & Wyman Ltd, Reading, Berkshire.

just
THE
JOB

CONTENTS

JUST THE JOB!

The *Just the Job!* series ranges over the entire spectrum of occupations and is intended to generate job ideas and stretch horizons of interest and possibility, allowing you to explore families of jobs for which you might have appropriate ability and aptitude. Each *Just the Job!* book looks in detail at a popular area or type of work, covering:

- ways into work;
- essential qualifications;
- educational and training options;
- working conditions;
- progression routes;
- potential career portfolios.

The information given in *Just the Job!* books is detailed and carefully researched. Obvious bias is excluded to give an even-handed picture of the opportunities available, and course details and entry requirements are positively checked in an annual update cycle by a team of careers information specialists. The text is written in approachable, plain English, with a minimum of technical terms.

In Britain today, there is no longer the expectation of a career for life, but support has increased for life-long learning and the acquisition of skills which will help young and old to make sideways career moves – perhaps several times during a working life – as well as moving into work carrying higher levels of responsibility and reward. *Just the Job!* invites you to select an appropriate direction for your *own* career progression.

Educational and vocational qualifications

A level – Advanced level of the General Certificate of Education

AS level – Advanced Supplementary level of the General Certificate of Education (equivalent to half an A level)

BTEC – Business and Technology Education Council: awards qualifications such as BTEC First, BTEC National Certificate/Diploma, etc

GCSE – General Certificate of Secondary Education

GNVQ/GSVQs – General National Vocational Qualification/ General Scottish Vocational Qualification: awarded at Foundation, Intermediate and Advanced levels by BTEC, City & Guilds, Royal Society of Arts and the Scottish Qualifications Authority (SQA)

HND/C – BTEC Higher National Diploma/Certificate

International Baccalaureate – recognised by all UK universities as equivalent to a minimum of two A levels

NVQ/SVQs – National/Scottish Vocational Qualifications

SCE – Scottish Certificate of Education, at **Standard** Grade (equate directly with GCSEs: grades 1–3 in SCEs at Standard Grade are equivalent to GCSE grades A–C) and **Higher** Grade (equate with the academic level attained after one year of a two-year A level course: three to five Higher Grades are broadly equivalent to two to four A levels at grades A–E)

Vocational work-based credits	NVQ/SVQ level 1	NVQ/SVQ level 2	NVQ/SVQ level 3	NVQ/SVQ level 4
Vocational qualifications: *a mix of theory and practice*	Foundation GNVQ/ GSVQ; BTEC First	Intermediate GNVQ/GSVQ	Advanced GNVQ/GSVQ; BTEC National Diploma/Certificate	BTEC Higher National Diploma/ Certificate
Educational qualifications	GCSE/SCE Standard Grade pass grades	GCSE grades A–C; SCE Standard Grade levels 1–3	Two A levels; four Scottish Highers; Baccalaureate	University degree

INTRODUCTION

Do you want to work with people? If the answer is *Yes*, stop for a minute to think just what you mean by that.

Almost every job involves working with other people, and it's hard to name a job in which you don't come into contact with somebody at some time. You could sell things to people, lock them up, teach them, nurse them, entertain them, bring them meals. The possibilities are endless! What might suit you, and what do YOU mean by *'working with people'*?

Working with the public

Jobs in this group are for people who are sociable, outgoing, confident and happy to talk to strangers. You may give people a service, or try to sell them something, but you don't get involved in sorting out their personal problems. You may get to know certain people quite well, because you see them over and over again, or you may be in a job where there are new people to meet all the time. Most jobs require other skills besides being able to get on with people.

Caring for people or helping them with problems

These jobs involve a different, deeper sort of contact with people, and are mainly in health, education and social services. Some of them are about helping people who are ill or who have a particular problem. In others, you teach people, or care for them physically. It may involve being with the people you are helping for a long period of time.

You need to be an approachable sort of person, with an insight into the way people think and behave. You won't solve all the problems you meet, or get thanks from all the people you try to help, and some people will resent your 'interference'. But there is also a lot of satisfaction to be had, if you are suited to the work.

Community work

Working in the community means undertaking tasks that need doing on behalf of everyone. You serve and help people in the course of your work. In some jobs, you also have to deal with people who are law-breakers, or those generally acting against the interests of the community.

A lot of the jobs are quite similar to those in the previous group, and you would need many of the same sort of qualities to do them well. But you may also need to adopt an authoritative manner on occasions and, perhaps, to enforce the law.

Teamwork

Perhaps you'd like to work as part of a team, if you're a sociable type of person. You can get a lot of satisfaction and support that way. Of course, many jobs involve teamwork, so look for those where this is a particular feature.

What next?

Are you now more clear about what you mean when you say you want to work with people? Have you been able to identify your main 'job group' amongst the four which are described above?

In addition to the jobs described in this book, you will find other ideas, or more detailed information, in *Nursing & Therapies*, *Teaching* and *Working with Children* (in preparation) in the *Just the Job!* series.

COMMUNITY WORK

Community workers provide facilities or advice, helping to solve problems on behalf of particular individuals or groups of people. They may work for a local authority – in the social services department or in youth and community service – or they may work for independent bodies, such as charities. Some jobs in community work require a degree; others ask for no particular academic qualifications.

The sorts of jobs which are described as *community work* include:

- **wardens of community centres** offering leisure and educational provision of all kinds for residents of a neighbourhood: old people, young people, housewives, unemployed people, etc;
- **youth and community workers** in youth clubs and centres. Detached youth workers assist young people who, for one reason or another, are not involved with official youth organisations;
- **liaison officers** and advisers working in multi-racial communities;
- **playworkers** and playscheme organisers;
- **people working for rural community councils;**
- **lawyers** and other workers in community law centres;
- **counsellors** in young people's counselling and advisory services;
- **advisers** in housing advice centres;
- **community arts workers** including artists, dramatists, musicians, and administrators;

- **students' welfare officers** – perhaps based in a university to help with problems of accommodation, the law, finance, etc.

Traditional community work

There are many opportunities to work for, with and within the community in the more traditional occupations, such as the police service (the community police officer on the beat), the health services (the district nurse, health visitor and community midwife), adult education, public libraries, and the churches.

QUALIFICATIONS AND TRAINING

It is very difficult to generalise about qualifications and training for community work. Some posts may require no academic qualifications or formal training, while for others – e.g. in law advice centres – you need a degree or appropriate professional training. For many posts, academic qualifications are less important than personality – all are likely to emphasise attitude, approach and relevant experience. Resilience and diplomacy are particularly important qualities.

Community workers have to deal with all sorts of people. There may be problems in reconciling the needs of the community with the stance of the local council. Community workers, employed by the particular authority, may need to be diplomatic! Often, problems can only be solved with persistence and/or compromise.

As far as formal training is concerned, youth and community courses, and some courses offering social work training, can be particularly relevant. There are also a few degree courses at Honours level covering community studies, youth studies, urban studies, etc. Some degrees include options in community studies as part of courses in social studies, education, etc. Most courses require you to have two A levels, though mature

students may be exempted. Youth and community work college courses normally require five GCSEs at grade C.

It is important to have relevant experience – whether voluntary or paid – in areas such as counselling and advisory work (consumer advice, marriage guidance, Citizens' Advice Bureaux), social work, youth work and local politics.

Some typical job advertisements

Assistant Community Relations Officer – *Do you have the skill, experience and commitment needed to promote racial equality and eliminate discrimination? The Officer will undertake a wide range of* duties such as Education, Youth and Project Work. The applicant should have experience of working with ethnic minority groups.

Family Welfare Officer required by Council for Community Relations to lead a team of four workers offering support to women living in a hostel and in the community. Punjabi speaker preferred.

Community Play Organiser – A committed, experienced and enthusiastic professional is required by the Borough Recreation Department to promote children's play in the seven permanent play centres and the mobile holiday caravans. Preference will be given to candidates with appropriate qualifications and experience.

Assistant Nurseries Organiser – to assist in the running of the Committee for Community Relations' five nurseries and one playgroup, including development of existing anti-racist work demonstrating good practice in multi-racial nurseries. Background and good experience of under-fives work required, as well as experience of working with Afro-Caribbean, Asian and other ethnic minority communities.

Employment Development Worker – wanted for community employment project in Birmingham, to develop employment initiatives, especially cooperatives and small businesses in mainly Asian neighbourhood.

Detached Youth & Community Worker – Ethnic Minorities – Applications are invited from suitably qualified and experienced people for the above newly created post, to work in predominantly Asian communities. Candidates should be knowledgeable in all aspects of racial disadvantage, have strong organising ability and the expertise to become involved in the community, identify needs and devise strategies to encourage self-help and greater awareness of resources available.

Arts for Disabled People – A Development Officer required to launch new organisation. Experience in Arts/Administration/Community Work.

CARING WORK

This section is about work which involves caring for people in a practical way. Generally, you don't need a lot of qualifications to do these jobs, especially if you are an older applicant. For many of the jobs you need to be at least 18 years old, and mature people are always very welcome to apply.

What it takes
- Personality is very important – you need to get on well with people.
- You need plenty of common sense and initiative.
- You need to be a responsible and dependable sort of person.
- A driving licence can be a big help.

The following paragraphs outline the different possibilities for caring work. Later sections go into more detail.

Caring for children and teenagers
Childminding, fostering, playgroup organising
These have been put together in one group as they are possibilities which are particularly suitable for people who have to stay at home. They are not very rewarding in financial terms, but are certainly a good way to gain experience of work with children. Many of the people who are attracted to this kind of work are raising, or have raised, their own family. See the next section, on Working with Children, for more information.

Nursery nurse and nanny

Nursery nurses and nannies care for children from birth up to about seven years old – washing and changing them, feeding them, playing with them, teaching them basic skills such as dressing and toilet training, and perhaps caring for their clothes. You can work in private houses, day and residential nurseries, nursery and infants schools, hospitals, and homes for children (including children with disabilities).

Playwork and adventure playground work

Some local authorities and voluntary organisations employ play-workers to help parents and children with play activities for pre-school children, to run after-school playschemes or to organise play sessions for children during holiday times. People with nursery nursing or teaching qualifications could go into this sort of work, as well as those with other appropriate experience of working with children.

Residential child care

Care assistants work in homes and residential special schools for children, fulfilling the same sorts of duties as a nursery nurse, but including more domestic work. Care assistants need not necessarily live in.

Childcare officers and **houseparents** are supervisory staff in homes and special schools. They are generally older, experienced people; the work is often residential, but not necessarily so.

Educational support work

Education support assistants deal with children of school age who are having difficulties at school for one reason or another. They also enforce attendance at school, and deal with truancy problems. They work closely with parents, teachers and other social workers.

Other opportunities

Most jobs in **schools** (teaching and non-teaching) involve opportunities to care for children. School secretaries and midday supervisory assistants are always plastering cut knees and listening to children's problems.

Voluntary work also presents opportunities for caring for children, especially deprived or disabled children.

Accommodation wardens can also get involved in welfare work with young people.

Caring for elderly people
Care assistant

Care assistants work in day centres and residential homes for elderly people. They provide care and help with all the everyday things like getting about, dressing, bathing, mealtimes and entertainment – anything to make the home or centre a happy and pleasant place. An encouraging, cheerful and practical outlook is needed, as well as a lot of patience and sympathy: it's not easy being old and unable to do things for yourself. For this work you must normally be over 18 and mature applicants are welcomed.

There are full-time college courses leading to GNVQs in caring skills which could give you a preliminary training, and part-time training with assessments for NVQs for people already in these jobs.

In some areas, **'domiciliary' care assistants** are employed to help elderly people in their own homes. These are people who are basically well, but need assistance with things like getting up and dressing for the day, bathing, getting themselves to bed, etc. They may come under the home carer service – see below.

Home carer

The social services department can provide home carers (formerly called home helps) for people of any age, but most of the work is with elderly people. The work depends on the needs of the individual client. It might be general cleaning, ironing, cooking a main meal, shopping or personal care. You need to be cheerful, practical and adaptable – and willing to face all sorts of situations. Some older people and their homes may be so neglected that the home carer has to sort out filthy conditions. Besides working for the social services, home carers can work as private helps or for voluntary agencies.

Other opportunities

There are plenty of opportunities for doing voluntary work with elderly people. You could just do this on your own initiative (shopping for neighbours, keeping them company, etc). Or, you could help through a national or international charity such as Age Concern or Help the Aged.

Accommodation wardens in elderly people's flats or group dwellings may get involved in caring to a limited extent.

Social and medical caring work

Social work assistant

Social work assistants can be involved with people of any age and with all types of problems. They are employed by local authority social services departments to work as assistants to professional social workers. They do not have sole responsibility for cases, but, under the direction of a social worker, interact with clients to find out exactly what problem a person or family has. They then assist in working out an action plan to help cope with, or resolve, the problem. They might sort out the resources needed to deal with a problem, perhaps enlisting other agencies' help. They must also be on the watch for social needs

18

within their area, and make these known to their team leader. There are various part-time training courses leading to NVQs for people doing this sort of work. With the right qualifications and experience, you could train as a social worker.

Nurses and healthcare assistants

You can take a general nursing training to work in ordinary hospitals, or specialise in nursing people with mental illness or disability. A nurse needs to be caring and able to work well in a team. Training takes three years. The minimum age is $17\frac{1}{2}$ and mature applicants are welcomed. Younger applicants should offer five GCSEs at grade C, and there are also training opportunities for those with A levels, Advanced GNVQ or degrees.

Healthcare assistants work in hospitals as assistants to the nurses, and need the same sort of personal qualities. They help with serving meals, feeding and bathing patients, bedmaking, etc, but they don't undertake medical duties. On-the-job training may be available. The usual minimum age is 18; mature people are welcomed.

Hospital porters and ambulance staff

Being taken into hospital when you are ill, getting transport to a day centre when you are afraid of falling or being jolted, being moved for treatment after an accident, going to the operating theatre – these are situations where a cheerful, careful and sympathetic porter or ambulance attendant can make all the difference. You have to be fit and reasonably strong to lift people. For ambulance work, a driving licence is usually required. You also need an interest in first aid and medical matters, as during your training you will learn to deal with medical emergencies. The minimum age is 18.

Other opportunities

Any 'medical' job involves caring for people: think of the work of a doctor, dentist or hospital receptionist; occupational therapist or physiotherapy aide; foot-care assistant, and many others. Accommodation wardens working with people with mental or physical disabilities are also involved in caring work.

Some recent job adverts in caring work

These will give you an idea of the sort of jobs you may see advertised locally:

Care Assistant *required by the local health authority to join a team of staff caring for a small group of children with special needs, living in an ordinary house. Our children require maximum care, therefore an essential requirement is an ability to establish genuine relationships with children. Applicants should be car owners and drivers.*

Home Care Organiser *with the Social Services department, to assess clients' needs, match services to clients, and manage a group of home carers, including recruitment. The post calls for managerial skills, tact, diplomacy and care for people. Car driver required.*

Non-resident Care Officer *needed by Social Services department for a children's home which offers an assessment facility. Requires an understanding of the special needs and problems of children separated from their families. All staff participate in rostered sleeping-in duties, for which an allowance is paid.*

Support Assistant *required by primary school to assist a child with special needs. 10 hours per week, term-time only.*

Scheme Assistant *for a housing scheme for 16 discharged mentally ill people. The Scheme Assistant will, under the supervision of the Scheme Manager, help to provide competent, tactful care and support to residents to enable them to maintain and extend their domestic skills. Previous experience with mentally ill people is not necessary, but the successful applicant will need to be patient and caring.*

Outreach Worker for Drugs Advisory Service *– to establish contact with drug-users at risk of HIV infection and AIDS, particularly within rural areas of the district. Own transport is essential.*

WORKING WITH CHILDREN

There are lots of jobs involving contact with children, besides being a nursery nurse, a primary school teacher or a nanny. For some of these jobs, exam qualifications may not be important and you could start at sixteen, while, for others, it may be necessary to follow a higher education course after A levels or equivalent.

All the jobs listed below can involve working with children in some way. The work is open to people of both sexes. Not all those on the list are open to young people at the age of sixteen, but they could still be kept in mind as possibilities for the future.

Note: Many applications for jobs involving contact with children require a police check on your background.

General childcare and community work
Au pair/parent's help
Some families employ au pairs and parent's helps to assist in the running of the household and to help to look after children. Although a college training is increasingly required, these posts are sometimes available to untrained people who, perhaps, have some paid or voluntary experience of looking after babies and children. Sometimes they offer suitable opportunities to gain experience before going on to train as a nursery nurse or as a residential care assistant.

Childminders and foster-carers

Childminders use their own homes to care for babies and children below school age, usually while their parents work. The parents pay the childminder an agreed weekly or hourly rate, and a good minder acts very much as a parent-substitute. He or she gives the child all the physical care, creative play and emotional comfort which are needed. There are legal regulations covering childminding, which set the limits on the number of children you may mind and the health and safety requirements. There is no requirement for minders to have any qualifications, though colleges of further education often run useful part-time courses for childminders. Most minders have plenty of practical experience from bringing up their own children.

Fostering is not exactly a job – but it can be a full-time occupation, and you are paid an allowance for the children in your care. Fostering arrangements are made by the social services department, who will discuss the whole matter with you and decide whether you are suitable to add to their register of foster-carers. There is a great need for long- and short-term foster homes for babies and young children, and also for teenagers. Caring for children whose normal routine may have been severely disrupted by a death or illness in the family, or who have been abused or neglected at home, is very demanding work. The social services staff would discuss all such aspects with you very carefully.

Nannies and nursery nurses

Nannies and nursery nurses work mainly with babies and children below school age. They are responsible for their general care and development. Nannies work for private families, either living in, or coming daily to look after the children. Nursery nurses work in day nurseries, residential homes, maternity or children's wards in hospitals and, very occasionally, in situations such as on board ship. It's not essential to have been trained to work as a nanny, but more and more advertisements ask for nursery nurse or similar qualifications.

Playgroup supervisors and playworkers

Playgroup supervisors, with help from parents, run playgroups for pre-school children. These are mainly run only in the mornings. There may be a small salary, but some playgroups are run just by volunteers. Besides the sort of playgroups which are run in church halls and community centres, you can also set up a playgroup in your home, charging a fee for each child who attends. To do this, you have to meet the health and safety requirements of the local authority social services department.

Playgroup supervisors often do not have any formal training before they start, but, once they have a job, they usually attend courses which are run by the local authority and the Pre-school Learning Alliance. The normal background is to have brought up a family yourself, though a person who has done a nursery nursing or similar training might be considered.

Playworkers work mostly with school-age children in adventure playgrounds or with after-school clubs and holiday playschemes.

Residential child care

Residential children's homes are places where children and young people live if they cannot stay with their own families. There are also opportunities in residential assessment centres, which cater for youngsters who may have a wide range of problems. The aim is to find the best sort of long-term help for them. Most of the children in homes and assessment centres are in the 10 to 18 age range, as younger children are generally put in foster homes.

Childcare staff work as part of a team, helping with the practical tasks of everyday living, and meeting the young people's emotional needs. This is done by trying to build up a caring relationship with each young person, and by providing appropriate rules and discipline.

Some homes specialise in caring for children with disabilities, and here the staff encourage each child's independence and try to develop the skills which are needed to cope with everyday life.

You must normally be over 18 to do this kind of work, and mature applicants are welcomed. Training is available for people to work towards NVQs at levels 2 and 3 in residential support and child care. There are also various full-time courses in care skills at local colleges, leading to Intermediate and Advanced GNVQs, which you might take in preparation for this sort of work. Senior staff are usually qualified social workers.

Nursing children with disabilities

Although this is really a medical job, nursing children with disabilities involves a lot of general care work too. Children with special needs are often resident for a time in special schools and hospitals, and they need nurses who have been specially trained to care for them. Children's nurses could work with physically disabled children, but there is special training available for nurses of people with learning disabilities. Both kinds of work demand a tremendous amount of patience. It may take months or years to teach patients even simple skills.

Part-time and voluntary work

This can be a valuable way of obtaining experience with children while you are still at school or college. Experience of this sort could be very useful in helping you decide whether you enjoy working with children and young people. It could also help you later on to get a place on a training scheme, or a job.

You could consider: babysitting; work with Brownies, Beavers, Cubs, Sunday School groups, etc; helping in a home or hospital; helping with an after-school playgroup for children of primary school age; a holiday scheme – e.g. an adventure playground project.

Teaching
Educational support assistants and escorts
Support assistants work in schools as helpers to particular children who have special educational needs. More and more, such children are now educated in mainstream, rather than special, schools. Support assistants can also help the teacher in a more general way with classroom activities. They can be employed in special schools, or in schools where there is a particular difficulty, such as a high percentage of infants who don't speak English. Each job is different. A child with hearing loss may need an assistant to interpret what is being said in the classroom. With a physically disabled child, the job might entail pushing his wheelchair from room to room, and helping him at lunch and with going to the toilet.

Escorts usually work for just a couple of hours a day, to help children with disabilities on their journey to school and back. That might mean a local journey undertaken every day. Or it might mean travelling further afield, but just on Mondays and Fridays if the child is a weekly boarder at a special school. Most of these jobs are part-time only, and you get school holidays, which makes them very popular! Mature applicants are welcomed.

Teaching in state schools
Teachers train to teach children within particular age ranges: nursery (three to five), infants (five to seven), juniors (eight to eleven), or secondary. Teaching three-year-olds obviously

requires a very different approach to teaching ten-year-olds. Generally, in schools for children under eleven, teachers spend most of their time with a particular group of children teaching them all subjects – from reading to technology. Intending teachers have to obtain a degree-level qualification.

Teaching in private schools/kindergartens

While there is no requirement for teachers in private schools to have a recognised qualification, in practice, most will have undergone teacher training.

For work in the kindergartens (nursery schools) run according to the educational principles of Maria Montessori, there are special training courses. Entrants would be expected to be of GCSE standard, but are considered on their individual merits. These courses do not provide acceptable qualifications for teaching in state schools.

Teaching a special skill – music, dance, etc

People with a particular talent, such as playing the piano, or ballet, may decide to teach their subject privately – i.e. to children who pay for lessons outside school hours (after school and on Saturdays, usually). Anyone can set themselves up as a private teacher, without special training, but, usually, high-level qualifications are obtained. It is also possible to teach special skills, such as playing the violin, to children in schools as part of their normal education. Peripatetic teachers travel around several schools in an area, giving lessons to small groups of children. These teachers must have a recognised teaching qualification in their specialist subject.

Medical jobs and work in the health services
Nursing, health visiting and midwifery

The nurse training programme allows specialisation after eighteen months of the three-year course, so it is at this point that students can opt to specialise in sick children's nursing. If you are already a registered nurse, you can take a further course. Training to nurse people with learning disabilities would also involve work with children (see above).

There are various ways to train in midwifery – the usual route is a three-year course, as part of the nurse training system. Already qualified registered nurses can take an extra 18-month course. It is also possible to do a three- or four-year degree course. Qualified midwives deal with unborn and very young babies (care of the pregnant mother, delivery of the baby and care of its mother in the first days of life).

A qualified adult nurse can become a health visitor, whose work is in the community and includes parentcraft advice and teaching, health education, and involvement in social as well as health problems. Besides work in hospitals, a qualified general nurse could work as a school nurse or matron, or in children's health clinics.

Doctors

Doctors can specialise in paediatrics (child medicine) or in school and community health services, dealing with children of all ages from birth (and pre-birth) to school-leaving age. General practice as a family doctor also gives plenty of scope for work with babies and children.

Dentistry

Dentists choosing to work with children can be employed by the school dental service or the maternity and child welfare service. Certain specialist careers, such as orthodontics (correction of irregularities in teeth), also involve much work with children. General practice in dentistry normally consists of a great deal of work with children as well as with older people.

Dental therapists, **dental hygienists** and **dental nurses** also have considerable contact with children.

Physiotherapy and occupational therapy

These therapists rarely work solely with children – though there is some scope for specialisation in special schools and hospitals.

Speech therapy

Speech therapists can work with people of all ages, but much of their work is with children. They help people with speech impediments, such as stuttering, to overcome their disability, and they treat patients who have speech defects arising from physical problems such as deafness or brain damage. Patients are treated individually or in groups – in clinics and schools.

Orthoptics

Orthoptists work under the supervision of a doctor to correct eye defects such as squints, 'lazy eye' and double vision. Most of their work is with children, and is carried out in schools, clinics and hospitals.

Audiology

Audiologists test hearing – both in adults and in children. Assessing the hearing of young children is a large part of the job. People who are discovered to have hearing difficulties are fitted with aids by the audiologist, who also instructs them in their use.

Jobs helping children and parents who have social problems

Social work

Work with children and families can form a large part of the social worker's caseload. There is some scope for specialising in work with particular age groups or types of problem, but experience of general social work would normally be required initially.

Childcare officers and **houseparents** work with children who cannot live with their natural families because of family difficulties, behavioural problems or disabilities. Voluntary organisations, and charities such as the NSPCC, Scope and the Children's Society, also employ professional social workers and care assistants.

Psychology

Child psychologists and educational psychologists are involved with children who have learning or behavioural difficulties because of social or emotional problems. They work with children and their parents.

Jobs offering general contact with children
School secretarial work

School secretarial staff often have a lot of contact with the children – dealing with day-to-day requests and problems. Experience in office work would be a normal requirement for this type of job.

Library work

Librarians and library assistants can sometimes specialise after training in children's books, or even libraries for toys. The **mobile librarian** or assistant, visiting rural neighbourhoods, might have some contact with children. Work as a **school librarian** or library assistant is also a possibility, and this would certainly involve getting to know the children and helping them to find information.

Shop work

Toy-shops, shops for babywear and children's clothes, shoe-shops, sweet-shops, some bookshops – all these offer possibilities for contact with children as a feature of the work. In a shop, you can work as a sales assistant, or as a trainee manager or manageress.

Other possibilities

Domestic work – in day schools and boarding schools, children's homes.

Work in holiday camps – often seasonal.

School ancillary work – support assistant, school meals staff, midday supervisor, school-crossing patrols, caretaking.

Jobs in entertainment – theatre, pantomime, radio and TV, etc.

Photography – possibility of specialising in child portraiture and school photographs.

Air cabin crew.

Swimming baths/sports centre work – including instruction.

Riding instruction.

YOUTH WORK

Youth workers help young people to develop their skills and qualities to the full, both as individuals and as members of society. They try to make sure that the same opportunities exist for all. Youth work may be done voluntarily or as paid employment. Professional youth workers have usually had previous experience as a volunteer, or as a part-time worker.

Usually, young people get involved with the youth service simply because they want to – to meet friends, to get out of the home for a while, to take part in some special activity, or to get help with a particular problem. Youth workers work with different age groups – the youth service is open to all young people aged between 11 and 25, with a special emphasis on the 13–19 group.

Youth workers are employed mainly by local authority education departments. There are also opportunities in projects concerned with information, advice and counselling for young people, or with voluntary organisations such as the clubs run full-time by the YMCA or YWCA. The majority of youth work in Britain is part-time, so full-time jobs can be difficult to find. It is worth considering getting a degree or qualification for a broader occupational area, or different job, before starting youth work training – if that is the area in which you still definitely want to work.

Youth work in clubs and centres

It isn't easy to define youth work in clubs and centres. Youth workers respond in a variety of ways to the needs of young people as they pass through adolescence to adulthood. The emphasis of the work in a particular post will depend on a number of factors, such as the social structure of the community, and whether it is located in a rural or urban area.

What the work involves

The work can include:

- organising activities to challenge young people in various ways, such as taking part in the Duke of Edinburgh's Award scheme;
- organising social and sporting activities for club members;
- working with unemployed young people;
- organising events away from the club premises;
- administering and managing the finances of the club;
- dealing with structural maintenance and general upkeep of the centre;
- recruiting and training voluntary workers;
- assisting and advising at smaller clubs which do not have a professional worker;
- liaising with professional and voluntary groups interested in the welfare of young people;
- individual counselling of young people;
- encouraging the involvement of young people in their community;
- organising international exchanges of young people;
- marketing the use of the club/centre facilities, locally – perhaps by other groups;
- assessing and responding to the leisure requirements of young people in the area.

Youth and community work in other settings

Many youth workers operate outside youth centres in order to reach young people who choose not to make use of clubs. Jobs include:

- youth work posts in the leisure industry, which may be based in a youth centre, a wing of a school or a sports centre;
- 'detached' youth work – i.e. working with young people who, for one reason or another, are not in contact with other agencies. Workers have to make themselves available in the places where these young people go – in cafes, pubs and on the streets;
- youth social work, in local authority social services departments. This may involve setting up community-based care for young people at risk of becoming seriously involved in criminal activity;
- helping young unemployed people to occupy their time usefully;
- young volunteer organisers – assisting young people who want to do voluntary work in the community;
- joint teacher/youth work jobs, often called 'youth tutor' posts, and others which carry responsibility for adult education as well as youth work, e.g. in community centres.

CAREER PATHS IN YOUTH WORK

There are no clear routes for career progression. Youth workers have to expect to move to gain promotion. It is a small profession, and there are few promotional possibilities available, even in work with the larger authorities.

What it takes

Youth workers come from a wide variety of backgrounds, and personalities are just as varied.

- They need to relate easily to young people and adults of all types.
- Youth workers must be able to encourage part-time and voluntary staff to develop their work.
- An interest in sport and/or an outdoor, artistic or musical activity is always valuable to youth workers.

- Youth workers liaise closely with the management committee of their centres, and have to cope with all the administrative work involved. They are responsible for all the resources – finance, buildings and equipment, as well as staff and members – and must be good organisers.
- The work can greatly affect your own social/family life. Evening and weekend work is essential – there are no set hours as such!

Kate – youth worker

‘ I started as a volunteer in my local youth club to see if it was something I really wanted to do. I am now a part-time paid youth worker, which combines well with my part-time piano teaching. I see my piano pupils during the day, which leaves evenings and weekends free for my youth work. If I ever want to be a full-time youth worker in a senior position, I shall need to get qualified.

What I love about the job most of all is being around young people. They have so much energy, which I like to think rubs off on me! I organise a lot of activities with them, particularly sporting ones. Two girls are currently going for their Duke of Edinburgh's Gold Award, and I'm helping them to achieve this.

I find the administration of the youth club a bit of a pain, as I don't like paperwork very much – nor the financial side of things. However, one of the older boys is showing a keen interest in this side of the club, and I am thinking about giving him some responsibility for this. I may get him to help me organise a camping trip for the club in the summer, which will involve quite a bit of administration before we go.

Some of the members can be a problem if they get in

trouble with the police, or fall out with their parents. I invest a good deal of time in building up good relationships with the young people in the youth club, as then they come to me with their problems instead of brooding on them. We often sit down and talk things through over a cup of coffee.

TRAINING

For most full-time posts with local education authorities, and also with many voluntary organisations, it is necessary to have a qualification recognised by the National Youth Agency. There are some posts for unqualified youth workers, but such opportunities are extremely limited.

The content of the different types of youth work training courses varies. Applicants should study prospectuses carefully to find the most appropriate courses for their needs. Special interests can be pursued, such as working with young unemployed people, or youth work in multicultural settings. All courses involve a large amount of practical work with placements in youth clubs. The academic side of most of the courses includes study of human growth and development, social psychology, sociology, social policy, education, counselling, and the principles and practice of youth work, including staff management and administration.

Courses acceptable to the National Youth Agency
Certificate or Diploma in Youth & Community Work (two years) – five GCSEs at grade C (or the equivalent) are the usual minimum entry requirement, although all colleges are prepared to consider applicants with lower qualifications if they have had relevant experience. Except where stated, the minimum entry age is 21. It is uncommon for trainee youth workers

to be over 45. Contact the NYA for a current list of courses offered (see Further Information section). LEA awards are available for some courses. Contact your local grants and awards department for further information.

Postgraduate courses for holders of any degree – competition for places is severe and relevant part-time or voluntary experience will greatly assist. The NYA will provide information on the availability of courses.

DipHE/first degrees – there are several courses in youth and community work which are designated as DipHE (Diploma of Higher Education) or degree courses. Studies at this level qualify the student for a mandatory grant. Consult the *Compendium of Higher Education* for a list of the universities and colleges which have professional endorsement from the National Youth Agency.

Other recognised qualifications and training

There are also various other types of qualifications currently recognised as being equivalent to youth work training. These include teachers who qualified before the end of 1988; and holders of some social science degrees and diplomas, providing the course has included appropriate youth and/or community content, together with a period of supervised relevant practical work. Teachers who qualified in or after 1989 will have to take further training, such as a one-year postgraduate course. The National Youth Agency considers applicants with such qualifications on an individual basis.

There is also an increasing number of part-time and distance learning opportunities leading to professional qualifications. Further information can be obtained from the National Youth Agency.

EDUCATION WELFARE OFFICER

The Education Welfare Officer's job is to make sure that all children benefit fully from education. They are really doing social work in an education setting, and are often called Education Social Workers. The qualifications requested by employers vary, but the Diploma in Social Work is usually required.

Education Welfare Officers (EWOs) still have their traditional job of dealing with problems of non-attendance at school by children under the statutory school-leaving age, and, where necessary, they prosecute parents whose children persistently stay away from school. But, generally, their role is now much wider than this.

What the work involves

EWOs are concerned with children whose family difficulties, which may be social, emotional or financial ones, give rise to behavioural problems or under-achievement at school. Generally, EWOs have responsibility for a school or group of schools in a particular neighbourhood. They make sure that families who should be getting help – such as free school meals, clothing, transport – do receive such help. They also try to develop better links between home and school, working closely with parents, teachers and school psychologists, and with other agencies such as the social services department, the probation service and the careers service. Part of their work may involve assisting in decisions concerning the provision of suitable education for children with special educational needs.

Though EWOs are backed up by the legal system, they try, by persuasion and encouragement, to convince reluctant (and possibly resistant!) parents and children of the advantages of full-time education.

Supta – Education Welfare Officer with a local authority

' I started off by qualifying as a social worker, which took me a few years. With that qualification, I could have chosen to be a probation officer, working with offenders and prisoners and their families, or I could have worked mainly with hospital patients, old people or families. Instead, I decided to specialise in work with children. By working as an education welfare officer (often called an education social worker), I not only spend time with children, but also liaise with teachers, educational psychologists and parents to try to find out why a child has problems at school. I am usually called in if a child is not attending school or is not doing as well as expected in class.

I find I have to be enormously patient, as the children (and sometimes the parents too) often do not wish to speak to me. I have to spend a lot of time coaxing them and building up a good relationship, so that they begin to trust me. This often means seeing families in the evenings or at weekends, when they can all be there together.

At the moment, like all social workers, I have a huge pile of paperwork to get through. I have to attend a case conference at the end of the week, which means I must write a lot of reports and ensure all my records are accurate and up to date. A case conference can be difficult, as everyone is there who has a hand in helping the family, and we all put forward our own recommendations for the best way forward. It doesn't pay to be shy or nervous!'

What it takes

Maturity, sensitivity and the ability to deal tactfully and sympathetically with all types of adults and children are very important. Experience of working with people in a caring or supervisory role is very useful, as the work can be challenging and, at times, frustrating. However, the demands of the job are countered by the special rewards of working successfully with young people in difficulties.

Accurate record-keeping and report-writing are necessary skills. Traditionally, education welfare has been a job for an older person, but increasingly, younger staff under 25 are being appointed. Where an authority does not insist on social work qualifications, there are opportunities for people from a wide variety of backgrounds, including teaching, but different local authorities tend to emphasise different requirements.

QUALIFICATIONS AND TRAINING

To study for the Diploma in Social Work (DipSW), applicants under 21 years old are required to hold a minimum of two A levels, or the equivalent, plus at least three other subjects at GCSE grade C. Applicants over 21 may be accepted without these qualifications. Some relevant prior experience, such as working with people in a caring capacity, either paid or voluntary, is usually necessary. The course can be work-based or college-based, and involves a minimum of two years' study, although this can be flexible. Some courses, taking three or four years, lead to both a DipSW and a degree qualification.

CONDITIONS OF EMPLOYMENT

EWOs do not have a fixed working week. Hours can be both long and unsocial. There will be evening work and weekend work to do – visiting parents who are out during the day.

Overtime payments may be made for this. The annual holiday entitlement is approximately four weeks plus public holidays – it varies according to the grade of the post and length of service. During school holidays, EWOs carry out normal casework as well as the administrative work related to their duties.

PROSPECTS

Within education welfare itself, promotion prospects are not very great because of the relatively small number of staff employed in each local authority. However, there are higher-grade posts for senior and principal education welfare officers. To take full advantage of promotion prospects, it would be necessary to move to other parts of the country as jobs arose. Pay is comparable to other types of social work.

It is also possible to move into related occupations – such as the social services, youth service, careers service, probation service, or education administration. Entry to these occupations depends upon the required academic and/or professional qualifications being held, but EWOs who hold the DipSW would be in a better position for transfer to related social work jobs. As some of these services are larger in terms of the staff they employ, promotion prospects could be increased in this way.

CAREERS ADVISORY WORK

C areers advisers help people to make important decisions about their education, training and future career.
This is often called *vocational guidance*. Careers advisers may
work in local careers service companies, in schools, colleges
and universities, in special guidance units for adults and in
private vocational guidance agencies. Careers advisers may
work with clients of all ages. You need to have a qualification in guidance and counselling to do this work, usually at
a postgraduate level.

Careers guidance – what it means

Careers advisers aim to help clients to reach their own, well-
informed decisions about their future. They do not tell people
what to do or what job they are best suited to, but help to eval-
uate different courses of action and suggest opportunities for the
client to consider.

The work with individual clients involves interviewing them.
This really means having a purposeful conversation – with the
adviser doing more listening than talking – to establish what sort
of person they are and what their abilities, preferences and
priorities are.

The careers adviser's skills lie in encouraging the client to talk
openly in exploring his or her ideas. The adviser asks helpful
questions which will bring out the client's feelings, and listens
carefully for 'cues' – remarks the client makes which need to be
picked up and investigated further.

Careers advisers need to be good communicators, observant, and able to establish a relationship with people very quickly. An interest in psychology and human behaviour is important, together with an analytical mind and a good memory.

Careers advisers may use various tests and guides (often computer-based) to derive more information about a client. These often involve the client in spending an hour or two working through a series of questions. There are tests to analyse people's interests, aptitudes and abilities, and the results of these, when interpreted carefully, can improve the effectiveness of vocational guidance.

Besides being able to find out information about the client, the careers adviser must also know about educational, training and employment opportunities. Advisers keep in close contact with employers, trainers and educationists, and do a lot of reading, so that the information on which they base their guidance is up to date. They also have access to libraries of information and computer databases which are constantly revised so that obsolete material is weeded out.

The careers service

Local careers service companies are the biggest employers of careers advisers. The basic task of advisers is to help school and college students and young unemployed people with their decisions and plans for the future, by providing free personal guidance and information. The service also helps young people to find suitable employment with training, and much of this work is handled by associate advisers or officers, working with careers officers. There is also work with adults, particularly those in education or who have disabilities.

Recent legislation has removed the careers service from those services provided by local authorities. The Secretary of State for

Education and Employment contracts with companies to provide the statutory service in each area. These companies can be totally private, or partnerships – for example between local councils and Training and Enterprise Councils (TECs).

What the work involves

A careers adviser in a careers service spends a high proportion of the working week on casework – interviewing young people in local schools and colleges or at the careers centre, and perhaps talking to groups of young people with similar interests or problems, or within a similar age group, with the same decisions to make. The careers adviser monitors the progress of anyone having particular difficulties, interviewing them more than once if needed, and carrying out other follow-up work on their behalf.

Time may also be spent seeing parents and, in some cases, liaising with training managers, college staff, personnel officers, social workers and other professionals.

There is also report-writing and administration which has to be done in connection with casework – careful notes have to be kept so that the careers adviser knows where a client is in their planning. Many advisers now use laptop computers for administrative work – a practice which can free them from dependence on an office base. Quite a lot of time is spent in discussions with school and college staff, to agree a suitable level of provision for careers education and guidance, and to contribute to the smooth running of the system.

Another major task is keeping up to date with local and national trends in education, employment and training – visiting local colleges, employers and those in employment with training, reading information items and researching particular topics from time to time. The careers adviser may also be involved in organising occasional careers conventions, where young people

and parents can meet representatives from education, training and industry.

PROSPECTS

After a couple of years doing the basic work, careers advisers may move into specialist areas, such as guidance for young people with special needs (learning difficulties or a physical disability, etc), employment and training liaison, information work, work with ethnic minorities or work with sixth-formers and college students. There are also promoted posts which involve management responsibilities and supervision of the professional and clerical staff, as well as senior management positions, with responsibility for running the careers service in an area. Traditionally, promotion has often meant moving to another careers service company, by applying for advertised vacancies.

Joshua – careers adviser

❝ I qualified for this job by doing a one-year full-time course after several years working in industry. Many of my colleagues are graduates. It's very hard to describe a typical working day, as every one seems to be different. Today I was in a school interviewing year 11 pupils. I'd made appointments to see eight of them, but only six turned up, so I spent the spare time doing all the paperwork that has to be done. Some careers advisers have laptop computers and type in action plans and reports during the interview. I tend to write up my notes afterwards. I find my days in school very tiring, as I have to do a lot of careful listening. I try to get pupils to "open up" to me, to explore their ideas and then to discuss what they should do next. I only get two minutes between interviews, which just gives me time to draw breath! These days, most young people ask about further and higher education, because they know they'll stand more chance of getting a worthwhile job with good qualifications.

Tomorrow I'm visiting three employers. I quite enjoy this, as I get to see all different kinds of work. I once went round a tailor's dummy factory, which was fascinating. Even better was going round a nightclub – during the day! We have to visit as many employers as possible (in fact we all have target numbers to achieve now) so that we build up our knowledge of occupations and the local area. Then we are able to advise young people properly.

I also have to do the odd "duty" day in the office, to deal with any telephone queries and see any clients who turn up wanting help or advice. Any spare time is spent in the careers library trying to keep myself up to date, reading any journals or new information that has come in, or I spend it catching up on all the administration — the report writing and correspondence.

I enjoy meeting young people, and trying to help them to make decisions about their careers. One thing I don't enjoy so much is attending school parents' evenings, as they always seem to be on the evenings when I'm missing out on something more sociable!

TRAINING

There are now two routes to becoming qualified as a careers adviser:

- to be assessed in the workplace for National Vocational Qualifications at level 3/4 in Guidance work;
- to attend a full- or part-time course at a university.

The Advice, Guidance, Counselling and Psychotherapy lead body has now established the standards for NVQs, which can be awarded by LGMB/ICG (Local Government Management Board/Institute of Careers Guidance), City & Guilds, or SQA, at level 2 in Advice, or Guidance, or Counselling, and at level 3 and 4 in Advice or Guidance. The LGMB can supply a list of approved centres where NVQs can be awarded in these work areas. The NVQs are suitable for those who are presently employed in related work within a careers service, or for those doing paid or unpaid voluntary work in counselling.

The second route involves taking a one-year full-time course, or a two-year part-time course, leading to a Diploma in Careers Guidance, which are offered at various universities.

Courses are followed by a first year in employment as a

probationer. If you are under 25, you need to be a graduate, or near equivalent, to be accepted for a DipCG course. Older applicants, who are generally welcome, may offer other appropriate experience. Many applicants offer a couple of years' experience in industry or teaching. LEA discretionary grants may be available, or training awards from the Local Government Management Board. Careers services can take on trainees, paying them a salary during the course and offering them a job on completion, but opportunities are few. The LGMB can award a premium grant for in-service trainees.

Other work in the careers service
Employment and training assistants, also called *associate/assistant advisers*, who liaise between young people and employers or trainers, **information assistants/receptionists** and **administrators** are also employed by many careers services. These vacancies would be advertised locally. It may also be possible to work in careers information without a DipCG but with relevant experience.

University and college careers services
Higher education establishments offer careers advice and help in finding vacancies for their students, most of whom are on degree and higher diploma courses. Besides the usual careers guidance functions – interviewing students, offering tests and computer guidance systems when appropriate, providing information – careers advisers in higher education spend a large proportion of their time liaising with recruiters of graduates, and arranging meetings and interviews for final-year students to meet potential employers.

Many advisers in higher education have a background in industry, and vacancy advertisements (see the *Times Higher Education Supplement* and the *Guardian* education pages) often specify that they want an adviser with a particular specialism, such as science or engineering. Some careers advisers have a DipCG and a previous background in a local authority careers service, but, though valuable, the Diploma is by no means essential for this type of work. Other qualifications in counselling or related areas may also prove useful. Careers advisers and information assistants currently working in higher education can study for the diploma through distance learning.

Adult guidance services

A relatively recent development in careers advisory work has been the growth of special adult guidance services, offering careers and/or educational guidance (the difference between the two is really artificial, but some services make the distinction for administrative reasons). A variety of organisations may be involved in running new guidance systems, though they tend to be linked to colleges or careers services. Advisers or guidance workers in these services may again have a careers service background (and DipCG) or may have previously made their careers in education (especially further education) or counselling. Thus, various backgrounds and qualifications seem to be acceptable. Vacancies will be found in the educational and local press.

School careers coordinators

Virtually all secondary schools (both state and private sector) have a careers teacher or careers coordinator, who is paid a special allowance for this responsibility. They may be promoted from within the school, or vacancies may be advertised in the usual places for teaching posts. What careers teachers actually do varies considerably from one school to another.

They may coordinate careers teaching and guidance activities, acting as an administrator or initiator, rather than an adviser. Others may actually do little beyond keeping a basic careers library. Occasionally, and perhaps mainly in the private sector, there are posts where the emphasis is on offering individual guidance to pupils and students. Most careers teachers find that their allocated time for careers work is inadequate and end up spending a lot of their own time on careers tasks.

Training for careers teachers is patchy – there are some one-year and one-term full-time courses available (for qualified teachers only), but permission to train through one of these courses may not be forthcoming. There are also a number of part-time in-service courses and basic short courses. In-service training has improved because of the increased importance given to the place of careers education in the National Curriculum.

Private vocational guidance services and agencies

Some advisers work in private vocational guidance agencies. These may be one-person operations, or partnerships, and are generally based in the larger cities – especially in London and the south. Most agencies charge their clients quite substantial fees.

Careers advisers in private agencies tend to make extensive use of psychological tests. In fact, many advisers have a psychology background. Some may have higher education or local careers service experience, and may possess a Diploma in Careers Guidance. Occasionally, people employed elsewhere as careers advisers undertake some private work in addition to their salaried post.

Private agencies tend to offer a one-off, though in-depth, service to clients, which includes a programme of testing, a personal interview, and a written analysis and report which includes suggestions of career possibilities. There is little follow-up work and they do not generally provide an employment-placing service.

WORKING WITH ELDERLY PEOPLE

There are lots of jobs where you can work with elderly people. Most come into the broad areas of caring, social work and medical work. Whatever your level of qualifications and your particular interests, you should find something to suit you.

There are many openings for working with elderly people through the government training provisions for young people or adults, or through voluntary work. You might consider these options either as a substitute for a job, or as a way of getting experience before starting direct employment or a college training course.

Care assistant

Care assistants can work in homes for elderly people. Some are run by local councils; others are private homes. Most of the elderly people who go to live in homes are no longer able to manage on their own.

As a care assistant, the major part of your work involves seeing to the daily care of the residents. You help them with dressing, washing, bathing, at mealtimes and getting about. You also talk to them, listen to them and help to keep them interested in life. No special qualifications are usually needed, but experience gained through training or voluntary work is helpful in seeing whether you are suited to the work. See the next section for fuller details.

Outside training through employment, the usual age to start working in a home is 18 and there is often a preference for older applicants.

Social worker

Social workers are trained professionals working with people of all ages who need support to cope with aspects of their lives. Most social workers work for local authority social services departments. Apart from those who are based in day centres or residential homes, not many social workers spend all their time with elderly people. However, elderly people and their families are always on a general social worker's client list.

Social workers help older people to come to terms with the restrictions which their physical frailty or immobility place on them − like giving up their own homes. Or they might help someone cope with the loss of a wife or husband. Social workers also play a major part in identifying elderly people in the community who are at risk because of factors like poor housing, low income, or problems related to mental or physical illness. Besides council posts, there are also paid jobs with voluntary agencies specialising in the welfare of elderly people.

Social workers train for a Diploma in Social Work, which can be achieved by a number of routes − through a full-time college course, part-time study whilst in employment, as part of a degree course or DipHE, etc. School-leavers would normally need two A levels, or their equivalent, to start the course, but this requirement can be waived for mature entrants.

Social work assistants, as the name suggests, help professional social workers with the more routine aspects of their work, and they can be employed in a similar range of settings. Some part-time college training is available, but nowadays most training is employment-based. Social work assistant posts need less in the way of formal qualifications, and in-service training may be provided.

Home carer

Home carers provide basic domestic help, and often personal care, so that elderly people can continue to live at home. They also provide much-needed company and a 'watchful eye'.

Home carers and live-in housekeepers/companions can work on a private basis for individual elderly people or their families: nursing or domestic qualifications may be preferred.

The majority of home carers (home helps) are employed by social services departments and some voluntary agencies to work mainly with elderly people in their own homes, though they can also help mothers with new babies, physically or mentally disabled people and families who are in need of support and training.

No special qualifications are needed to be a home carer – it's more a matter of maturity, common sense and the right sort of personality to deal with elderly people, who can often be set in their ways and fiercely independent.

Home care manager/organisers are also employed by social services departments to administer the home care service and to make sure that high standards are maintained.

Besides paid work, helping people with jobs around their homes is frequently done as voluntary work by school and college students – and older people too. It's a good way to see how well you can get on with old people and their needs.

Health visitor

Health visitors are fully qualified nurses who have taken special training in aspects of community nursing. They are especially concerned with promoting good health and the prevention of

illness. Whilst much of the work of health visitors is with babies, pre-school children and their parents, they also work with elderly people. They try to make sure that older clients look after themselves properly so as to avoid the fairly common problems of malnutrition and hypothermia. Health visitors try to encourage the elderly to adopt a lifestyle that dispels loneliness. Their involvement can be with individual people in their homes, or in clubs and day centres. Referrals often come to health visitors through family doctors, with whom they work closely.

District nurse

District nurses are fully qualified nurses who have taken special training. This enables them to provide skilled nursing care to people in their own homes or in residential care. Their patients may have all sorts of health problems. Some are people who have just been discharged from hospital, those who have acute or chronic illnesses and those who are dying. While there is no real opportunity for district nurses to specialise in the care of elderly people, older people naturally form a high proportion of their patients. District nurses are normally based with a particular surgery or group practice, and care for the patients of that practice. They alert doctors, when necessary, to any change in a patient's condition. There are also jobs in the evening nursing service, which provides care for patients at home who are unable to put themselves to bed and who may need dressings attended to before settling for the night.

Other nursing opportunities

Nurses can specialise in the care of geriatric or elderly patients in wards of general or psychiatric hospitals and in other institutions, such as hospices (special-care hospitals for terminally ill people). Some will have taken specialist training in the care of elderly people, but it is not essential.

There are also openings for **healthcare assistants** in hospitals, performing work similar to that of care assistants in residential homes.

Nursing posts also occur within council and private residential homes for elderly people, and there are opportunities for nurses to work on a privately employed basis for individual elderly people and their families.

Doctor

Doctors work a great deal with elderly people, who typically occupy a large proportion of the time of general practitioners (family doctors). There are chances for doctors to specialise as consultants in geriatrics or psycho-geriatrics and to work in hospices. Many other specialist consultants have a high proportion of elderly people as patients -e.g. stroke victims, sufferers from respiratory troubles, people needing artificial joint replacements and so on.

Other health service opportunities

There are other occupations in the health services in which you meet a high proportion of elderly patients:

- **podiatry (or chiropody)** – specialising in foot care, either through private practice or the National Health Service;
- **occupational therapy** – working with people in their own homes, day centres, general and psychiatric hospitals to help them cope with the skills of everyday living;
- **hearing-aid dispensing** – ensuring that hearing aids and appliances suit the patient's hearing problems;
- **optometry and dispensing optics** – fitting patients with suitable glasses or lenses to correct visual problems.

Employment with charities

There are paid jobs with local and national charities which are concerned with the welfare of elderly people, including Age Concern and Help the Aged. Some jobs, such as social work posts, bring you into direct contact with elderly people in this country or overseas. In other jobs, there may be less personal contact with elderly people, but their interests are still involved, for example in fund-raising jobs.

Voluntary work

This can cover a large range of activities. Ideas include doing housework or shopping for less mobile elderly people in the community; gardening and decorating for them; helping with meals-on-wheels or books-on-wheels services; visiting old people to keep them company, in their own homes or in residential homes; reading to them and providing a 'good neighbour' service; getting up a group to provide entertainment in old people's clubs and homes. You can get involved in voluntary work either just through your own initiative (with people you know in your street or village) or, if you don't know where to start, ask your local social services department to give you some contacts.

Other ideas

These are just some ideas to get you thinking. Lots of other jobs can provide contact with elderly people if the work is done in a particular context. For instance, a hairdresser might specialise in doing older people's hair in their own homes, or in homes for elderly people – and could gain and give a lot of pleasure from the incidental chat with clients. Another person might offer day or evening classes in any subject which might appeal especially to older people – e.g. 'Coping on a pension' or 'Cooking for one'.

just
THE
JOB

CARE ASSISTANT
WITH ELDERLY PEOPLE

C**are assistants** give practical help and care to elderly
people in day centres, residential homes and nursing
homes. You can also work with elderly people in their own
homes, as a **home carer**, providing the support needed to
help older people to continue to live independently. You
do not need any particular qualifications to get started, but
can gain qualifications while at work.

The proportion of elderly people in the community is growing,
so you will often see jobs in residential or home care advertised.
It is important for carers to appreciate and respect the individual
circumstances and needs of the people in their care.

Residential care assistant
The work includes:

- helping the residents with their daily routine – getting up,
  getting washed, dressed and so on;
- serving food and perhaps assisting residents with eating their
  meals;
- helping to keep everyone occupied and happy, by talking or
  reading to residents, playing games and taking them on walks
  or trips;
- doing general domestic work, cleaning, tidying, making beds
  and washing up and encouraging residents to take part in
  these activities.

Some residents will need more help than others – particularly those who are confused or disabled. They may need assistance with moving in and out of wheelchairs, help with using the toilet and so on.

What it takes

To do this work, you would need to:

- be patient, sensible and responsible;
- like working with people – it helps to have a cheerful disposition;

- be healthy with the stamina needed for an active job;
- be prepared to work shifts (evenings and weekends), possibly with sleeping-in duties.

Michelle – care assistant in a residential home

I really like this job. The old people and the other members of staff are very friendly.

I have to get the residents on the first floor up in the morning, but most of them are awake already. I then have to take some of them to the toilet, which I don't enjoy, but it has to be done. You soon learn skills like how to help lift people properly, and you can gain qualifications in different aspects of the job while you work. I get quite hungry at lunchtime as I can't eat until I have served all the residents with their food. The afternoons are the best, as that's when we might take the more active ones out for a short walk, or even a visit to the shops. Sometimes we arrange for people to come in and provide musical entertainment.

What I really like is the time I spend chatting to the old people about when they were young, or writing letters for them. I get very fond of some of the residents, and it's so sad when one of them dies, but I like to think I've helped make life a little more pleasant for them.

TRAINING, QUALIFICATIONS AND JOB–FINDING

You will need to be at least 18 to do this work. Although educational qualifications are not necessarily required, a suitable course would be a good preparation. Further education colleges and some schools offer a range of courses, such as GNVQ in Health and Social Care. Find out what is available locally.

Various part-time and in-service training courses in social care are available for people employed as care assistants, to keep them up to date with new developments in the field of caring for elderly people. These courses often lead to National Vocational Qualifications. The Central Council for Education and Training in Social Work offers NVQs in Care at levels 2 and 3. These can be achieved while you are working. NVQ level 3 can be acceptable for entry to a Diploma in Social Work course if you want to train as a qualified social worker.

If you are offered a job, ask what training and qualifications will be available to you. School-leavers may be able to find appropriate training with an employer through work-based training – contact the careers centre for details. Adults are usually welcomed, especially if they have experience of caring for elderly relatives.

Day centres and some residential homes are run by social services departments, and there are many privately owned residential homes and nursing homes. Vacancies for care assistants are advertised in careers centres, Jobcentres and local papers. Addresses of local elderly people's homes can be found from your local social services department and in the *Yellow Pages* telephone directory under 'Residential and Retirement Homes'.

Home carer/community care assistant
The home care service provides vital support to people who need assistance to live independently at home. Clients may be of any age, with all sorts of different needs, but the vast majority of them are elderly people. A home visit is made to assess an individual's needs, and they are then assigned a home carer who calls in daily, twice weekly or as often as necessary.

As a home carer you would:

■ assist with washing and dressing your clients;

- help with domestic tasks, such as cleaning, washing, ironing, laying a fire;
- do the shopping, collect clients' pensions, prescriptions and other items.

What it takes

Home carers need to:

- have a cheerful, sociable disposition;
- be a listening ear, ready to give support;
- be happy to work unsocial hours: home carers often have to work weekends and evenings on a rota basis;
- be able to travel around to the different clients – a car is essential for some jobs.

TRAINING

Many local authority social services departments run their own training schemes for home carers, or they may use the in-service training courses mentioned above, leading to National Vocational Qualifications.

With experience you could progress to become a **senior home carer**, or **home care manager**, doing the weekly planning for your team of carers, reviewing each client's home care provision, etc.

ACCOMMODATION WARDEN

> The job of accommodation wardens is to look after residential hostels, such as halls of residence for students, YMCA/YWCA hostels, types of holiday/leisure accommodation – in the main, places for young people to live and stay. Other opportunities for wardens involve responsibilities closer to social work, such as in hostels for individuals with specific needs.

Throughout Britain, there are a very large number of halls offering accommodation to students during the academic terms at colleges and universities. These buildings all require wardens, who generally live on the premises. During the vacations, the rooms are let to conference members, delegates on short courses, former students or visitors to the region, so the warden is kept busy throughout the year.

The types of holiday accommodation where wardens are necessary include youth hostels, outdoor activity centres and campsites. Here, the work can involve contact with all age groups.

All the hostels run for single homeless people, former alcoholics and drug addicts, community houses for people with disabilities, and the sheltered housing for elderly people, need accommodation wardens present on the site. These types of hostels may be run by local councils, housing associations or charitable/voluntary organisations.

Most jobs involve 'living in', at least while you are on duty – and you may consider the accommodation which goes with the job as a perk. Many of the hostels for people pursuing leisure activities are located in attractive surroundings, such as the Brecon Beacons or the Lake District.

What the work involves

Obviously, the emphasis of the work will vary greatly according to the type of accommodation provided and the people it caters for. But, generally, it's a job which involves a lot of different responsibilities. These include:

- **housekeeping** – seeing that rooms are kept clean, bed linen changed, etc;
- **collecting money** – seeing that rents or fees are paid;
- **catering** – organising meals, seeing to communal kitchens;
- **welfare** – keeping an eye on residents, making sure that they

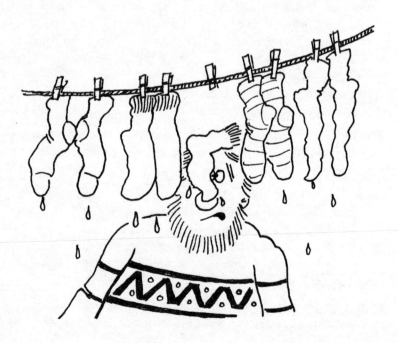

live together as harmoniously as possible, and dealing with any complaints.

Work mainly involving the catering and housekeeping aspects of providing accommodation is often known as 'catering services management', and the book on *Hospitality, Travel & Tourism* in the *Just the Job!* series tells you more about this.

If you work in a home or hostel for people with particular problems or needs, then the welfare aspect of the job will be the main one. You will get involved with your residents on an individual basis, and may spend a lot of your time helping them towards greater confidence and independence. For people with learning difficulties, this might mean teaching them how to cope with basic everyday tasks, like going shopping on their own, and cleaning and cooking for themselves. The warden in sheltered accommodation for elderly people has to be aware of the needs, health and safety, and general well-being of all the residents, and a nursing background is usually preferred.

What it takes
- good organising ability;
- confidence and self-reliance;
- ability to shrug off criticism if you have to make unpopular decisions;
- an approachable manner and a liking for working with people – but, in some jobs, you will also need an assertive manner at times;
- willingness to work unsocial hours;
- maturity – this isn't a job which you can do immediately on leaving school;
- previous experience and training in something like catering, youth and community work, social work or nursing, depending on the exact job.

No particular educational requirements are likely to be specified, but a good general education will help.

EMPLOYMENT

Positions as wardens of hostels are usually advertised locally in the newspapers and Jobcentres of the area. For jobs as accommodation wardens of outdoor pursuit or field study centres, youth hostels and recreation/leisure sites, look for advertisements in the quality newspapers and the *Times Educational Supplement*, which comes out on Fridays.

WORKING WITH PEOPLE WITH SPECIAL NEEDS

You may feel you would like to work with people with special needs. But perhaps you don't know what the work might involve or how to set about it. This section gives you an idea of the range of possible jobs.

Demanding work

One point needs to be stressed. If you tend to find relationships with the 'normal' world difficult or awkward, and feel that dealing with people who have disabilities will be easier, think again! Teaching a class of children with severe learning difficulties, for example, can be physically and mentally exhausting. Not only do you have to form relationships with the children, but also with their parents, social workers and other social agencies. It is not a job where you can shut yourself away with a group of people with whom you hope you can feel comfortably superior!

Ask yourself *why* you want to work with people with special needs and be sure you have a good answer. It will certainly be a key question at any interview for a job or training course.

Age limits

There are opportunities in this area both for young people and for older entrants. However, school-leavers will find there are few jobs they can go straight into. Some jobs have minimum age limits of 17 or 18, and a young person will often need to do some training or other sort of work first. Maturity and wider experience are often an advantage. Adults may find that, in view of their maturity and any previous experience, stated entry requirements to jobs and courses can be relaxed.

Types of jobs
Care assistant

Care assistants can work with people of all ages who have all sorts of disabilities – in residential homes, schools and in people's own homes. Their job is to provide basic everyday care. What that means obviously depends on the abilities of the people they look after. It might mean getting them washed and dressed in the morning, feeding them or helping them to feed themselves, dealing with toileting and generally helping them to get around and manage their daily activities.

You don't need to have any special qualifications to do this sort of work, nor to have taken any formal training before you apply for a job, but there are useful courses and qualifications you could take at colleges of further education – enquire locally. Depending on your age, you can get training and experience through employer-based training or a government-sponsored training scheme: ask at your careers service or employment services office.

You might be able to consider doing voluntary work. Some charitable bodies which run their own residential homes (such as Scope) also provide their own training. There are also residential communities for people with disabilities, such as the Camphill Villages and other Steiner-based organisations. Residents and volunteers share in all aspects of the community.

Care officer

In residential homes, hostels, etc, there are more senior staff, responsible for the overall running of the establishment and the welfare of residents. These staff generally have qualifications in care or social work. The Diploma in Social Work (DipSW) can be taken either by following a full-time college course or on a part-time basis while in employment.

Healthcare assistant

In hospitals and long-term care for people with mental or physical difficulties, staff are employed to help the nurses with mainly non-medical tasks. Normally, no qualifications are needed to do this work, and training is given on-the-job. There is usually a lower age limit of 18.

Nursery nurse

A nursery nurse can work with children in residential homes or in day centres, or as a nanny to a family. To become qualified, you need to take a two-year full-time college course (or part-time equivalent) leading to a NNEB Diploma in Nursery Nursing awarded by the Council for Awards in Children's Care and Education (CACHE). Young applicants require around three GCSEs at grade C.

Nurse

Trained nurses work with people with physical disabilities in a variety of situations – homes, hospitals, schools, etc. There are post-qualification courses open to nurses who want to specialise in this sort of work. To train as a nurse takes about three years, and requires a minimum of five GCSEs at grade C, although many applicants have higher qualifications. Mature applicants who don't have these exam passes can ask to take a special entrance test instead.

Learning disability nursing

This is one of the four branches of nursing in which people can specialise during the training described above. A major part of the job is helping patients to live as full a life as they can, in spite of their disabilities. Patients – both children and adults – normally need a lot of help and treatment over a long period of time.

Social worker

Social workers may work wholly or partly with clients with various disabilities, though in the first place they will take a general training. There are courses for graduates and non-graduates, and training can be employment-based or college-based. Younger people going into social work training normally need a minimum of two A levels/BTEC National Diploma/Advanced GNVQ, but adults can often be accepted with lower qualifications. (See next section.)

Social work assistant

Social work assistants help social workers with the more routine work. You may be able to get a post as an assistant on the strength of your personal experience rather than educational qualifications. There are also college courses which could be useful to someone wanting to do this sort of work. Once you have a job, you may be offered the chance to take a social work training and become qualified.

Psychologist

Psychologists who deal wholly or partly with disabled clients may be either *educational* or *clinical* psychologists. Both specialisms mean taking a psychology degree first (at least two A levels or an equivalent qualification are normally needed for entry), followed by further training.

Doctor

Doctors may choose to specialise after their initial training in some aspect of disability – such as surgery, psychiatry, audiology, ophthalmology or rehabilitation. To train as a doctor requires three very good A levels, usually in science subjects.

Instructor

Instructors work in employment rehabilitation and adult training centres with people who have either physical or mental disabilities, or a combination of the two. This is not a job for a school-leaver, but someone with practical skills and experience in an area like woodworking or engineering might well be able to do this sort of job. A very patient and sympathetic personality is essential.

Teacher

Teachers can specialise in teaching children with special physical, mental, sensory or behavioural needs. The usual training route is a BEd degree, or some other degree followed by a postgraduate certificate of education (PGCE). It is usual to gain experience teaching children who do *not* have special needs before going on to take a diploma course in special education.

Teachers in independent schools for children and young people with special needs may be expected to train in the particular approach of that school. There are Steiner schools, for instance, which operate according to particular principles, and teachers in these schools need not necessarily have a BEd or other DFEE-approved qualification (though many do).

To be accepted on a BEd or other degree course normally requires a minimum of two A levels or their equivalent, although this condition of entry may be relaxed for adult applicants. Teachers must have GCSEs at grade C or above in maths and English, and those intending to teach in primary schools now need GCSE science too.

Careers officer/adviser

Most careers services employ specialist careers officers/advisers who deal mainly with the employment and training problems of young people with special needs. Trainee careers officers/advisers are usually graduates, or mature entrants with relevant employment experience. There are also openings in careers advisory work with organisations such as Scope and the Royal National Institute for the Blind. (See separate section.)

Disability employment adviser

Disability employment advisers work at employment services offices or Jobcentres, offering a similar service to careers officers, but for older people. They normally enter the Civil Service as Executive Officers (two A levels or their equivalent are needed), and specialise after a few years' general experience.

Physiotherapists and occupational therapists

These may work partly or wholly with people with various disabilities which may be mental or physical, or the result of sensory loss (blindness/deafness). Degree courses normally require two A levels or their equivalent, preferably including a science.

At a lower level, physiotherapy and occupational therapy **aides** are employed to assist the professional staff. Qualifications are not normally specified for these jobs, which can be very suitable for mature people.

Speech therapist

Speech therapists may work with people suffering from hearing loss, learning difficulties or physical difficulties which cause speech problems. At least two A levels are normally needed to enter training.

Music and art therapists

A small number of music and art therapists work with people

suffering from mental or physical illnesses or disabilities, in hospitals and educational establishments. The usual qualifications needed to do this type of work are an appropriate basic training, followed by a diploma course in therapy techniques. This is an area in which charitable organisations, running homes and schools, may train their own therapists using a specific approach. Drama therapists, dance therapists, horticulture therapists and other specialists also work with people with various disabilities, though openings are rather scarce. (See section on creative therapies.)

Specialist worker with blind and partially sighted people

These might work within the community or with children in special schools, or as support workers in mainstream schools. There are specialist training courses, including degree courses, available.

The Public Information Service of the Royal National Institute for the Blind (RNIB) can provide information on volunteer work opportunities and careers with the RNIB and other associations assisting the visually impaired. An information pack on working with children is available from them.

Henshaw's College (see Further Information section) also provides training for work with visually impaired people, including short courses, flexible learning and a two-year full-time Diploma in Higher Education (Rehabilitation Studies). The latter is a professional qualification for would-be **rehabilitation officers**, whose job is to assess needs and then design, put into practice and monitor rehabilitation programmes. Their aim is to help the visually impaired client to achieve as much independence as possible, in terms of mobility, communication and lifeskills. Obviously, good communication skills are required, plus the ability to work in a team and liaise with other professionals.

Audiology technicians and hearing therapists

Audiology technicians measure patients' hearing and fit hearing aids and other appliances. Both audiology technicians and hearing therapists can give guidance. Lipreading teachers can also be trained to help adults who have lost their hearing.

Playworker

Playworkers can work as employees or volunteers in playgroups which are run specially for children with learning difficulties and/or physical disabilities. There are some full-time and part-time courses in playwork, and other sorts of training (for example, in nursery nursing or youth work) can also be appropriate.

SOCIAL WORKER

Social workers try to help individuals and families with problems, the roots of which may lie in illness, unemployment, poor housing, low income or old age. Helping people to solve their problems, or to come to terms with them, is not an easy job. A social worker therefore needs a good education followed by professional training, and the right personality.

Different types of social work

Social work can be either voluntary or paid. Voluntary work offers scope for many different activities: meals on wheels for local elderly people, providing hospital cars, taking disabled children swimming, work overseas in developing countries. Paid social work can be done at professional or assistant level. Most social workers are employed by local authority social services departments, but there are also opportunities for employment with charities and other organisations.

Social workers work in all types of communities, not just in run-down inner cities. Most deal with people of all types, ages and backgrounds – children, elderly people, families and single parents. Every case is different.

Most social workers now specialise in a particular type of work. They might concentrate on cases involving young children, adoptions and fostering arrangements; people who are mentally or physically ill; work in residential homes for children and young people who cannot live with their natural families. The current emphasis on community care means there is an increased amount of work with elderly and disabled people who might previously have lived in hospitals or residential homes. Their needs are assessed and plans for their care drawn up. Others work as education welfare officers, dealing with any problems which may prevent schoolchildren from getting the most out of their educational opportunities (see earlier section).

At present, probation officers are qualified social workers who specialise in working with young offenders and prisoners, and towards the rehabilitation of people who have served prison sentences (see later section). Besides those jobs which actually need qualified social workers, there are many others which are closely related to social work: youth workers working with young people from ethnic minorities; careers officers who choose to specialise with youngsters with special needs; community workers; play leaders; health visitors; church workers.

Satisfactions and drawbacks

Many people want to do some kind of social work because of a desire to help people in difficulties, but they do not always realise what a hard job it is. Social workers have rules and guidelines to follow in dealing with problems, but there may be no simple solutions to the situations which they meet. They often have to rely on their own initiative and on techniques learned during training. In some cases, there may be no long-term solution at all to a problem. Lack of funds, or a client's refusal to cooperate, may mean that an obvious solution to a problem can't be carried out. Then the social worker's efforts come to nothing. Much of social work is about helping people to cope with continuing problems, rather than finding a magical cure.

Some clients can be uncooperative, ungrateful and even violent, and the social worker who thinks he or she is going to change the world and solve every problem will be disappointed! People often regard social workers as either interfering do-gooders, or ineffective people who ignore things like early-warning signals of child-abuse. It's a very hard job to get right, and social workers often come in for a lot of criticism.

But there are, of course, many satisfactions too: sorting out a successful adoption, helping a family gain some stability after a difficult crisis, or helping an elderly person to carry on leading an independent life.

Not just client-contact . . .

Remember that, although it is very much a people-based job, there is also a lot of paperwork and administration to be done. There are records to keep, liaison with other organisations such as the Department of Social Security, the police, community workers and the education services. The social worker is often a go-between. Sometimes this means negotiating on behalf of the client – perhaps with the police, or to get welfare benefits, or to deal with a housing problem. But social workers themselves also become involved in legal procedures. They may have to take children into care – often against the wishes of the parents – and arrange the compulsory admission of mentally ill patients to hospital. There are also court appearances, when they give social reports on offenders.

What it takes

The work can be emotionally demanding. You must be able to appreciate your clients' problems without getting involved on a personal basis. You have to be tough enough and tolerant enough to put up with occasional abuse and lack of cooperation from clients, whilst still carrying on trying to help them. You also have to be very observant and not easily taken in. Press reports of cases of severe child abuse have shown up the awful results which can occur when social workers and other professionals do not recognise that all is not well with a child under their supervision.

As problems do not arise only during office hours, social workers often have to work in the evenings and at weekends.

Being able to drive may be expected – if you cannot drive, you'll certainly find that your choice of jobs is restricted.

PROFESSIONAL QUALIFICATIONS AND TRAINING

The Diploma in Social Work (DipSW) is the professional quali-fication for all social workers in the United Kingdom, in what-ever setting or sector they work. DipSW programmes require at least two years of full-time study, or the part-time equivalent, and supervised practice. The DipSW can be taken through a course of college-based training or through an employment-based route. Employment-based students are already employed in social services when they apply for admission to a pro-gramme. Admission is with the agreement of the employer. Students keep their jobs and continue to be paid a salary. The majority of DipSW students train on college-based programmes.

Students may choose to follow either a general pathway, or a particular pathway which gives the opportunity to specialise in a specific group of clients or type of service.

There are different types of DipSW programmes to cater for graduates, school-leavers and college-leavers with A levels or equivalent and non-graduates. Most DipSW programmes are full-time, but some offer part-time options and some are extended to make it easier for people with family commitments to undertake training. Distance-learning routes are also avail-able. About half of all entrants to social work courses are non-graduate, but many of these will be older entrants. If you are still at school or college and wondering which is the best route to take, note that promotion prospects are likely to be better with a degree. The route chosen will also depend on how committed you are to the idea of a social work career – obviously a degree keeps alternative career options open.

Degree programmes combined with DipSW

Various universities and colleges of higher education offer programmes leading to both a degree and DipSW qualification. These programmes last for three to four years. These are the most relevant for school- and college-leavers with a strong commitment to social work, but they are also appropriate to older applicants who are suitably qualified. Relevant work experience is usually required. Application is through UCAS. Mandatory awards are normally available through the local education authority.

Non-graduate DipSW programmes

These are two-year programmes which are often combined with a Diploma of Higher Education (DipHE). Applications for most full-time programmes are through the Social Work Admissions System (SWAS) – apply from September for programmes beginning a year later. You can apply for a local authority mandatory grant if the programme offers a DipHE with the DipSW. If the programme does not offer a DipHE you can apply for a local authority discretionary award, but these are limited. There are also some part-time and extended programmes for non-graduates; applications for these are sent direct to the institution concerned.

Postgraduate DipSW courses

If you already have a degree, or want to take a degree before making any firm commitment to a social work career, this is the route for you. Relevant work experience is required. Some programmes require a social science degree, but many programmes will accept a good degree in any subject. In exceptional cases, non-graduates with very substantial experience or other further education or professional qualifications may be considered. Postgraduate DipSW programmes last for two years. Candidates with a relevant degree may be able to negotiate credit exemptions with the programme. Some bursaries are available, but not for students wishing to specialise in education welfare work. You can obtain further information from the Central Council for Education and Training in Social Work (CCETSW). Application is through SWAS.

Please note: it is important to check that a DipSW programme has CCETSW-approved status: your qualification could be in jeopardy if approved status had not been granted by the time you finished your programme.

ENTRY REQUIREMENTS

An applicant to a DipSW programme must, in the opinion of the programme provider, be likely to succeed in completing the programme and be suitable to become a social worker.

All candidates under the age of 21 must have a minimum of two A levels plus supporting GCSEs at grade C. Equivalent qualifications would be a relevant BTEC National Diploma/Certificate, Advanced GNVQ or NVQ level 3. Certain Open University courses, Access courses or Nursery Nursing diploma may also be accepted as entry requirements. Universities will often require three A levels. The DipSW cannot be awarded to candidates under 22.

Candidates over the age of 21 are not required to have formal qualifications, but will be expected to demonstrate their ability to study at an advanced level.

Most DipSW programmes require candidates to have had work experience in social services or a related field. A minimum of one year's experience of either paid or voluntary work is often required, and the majority of successful candidates to social work training have between two and five years' experience.

PROSPECTS FOR SOCIAL WORKERS

A recent survey shows that demand for newly qualified social workers is high. Most students have the promise of a job before they qualify, and usually in the area where they trained. Jobs in community care are on the increase, while residential care is decreasing. To see the sorts of vacancies which occur for new and experienced social workers, look at the job adverts in the *Guardian* on Wednesdays – which you can buy, or read in your public library – also in *Community Care* and *Care Weekly*. Promotion prospects for experienced social workers are quite good, but, as in many professions, senior posts normally involve more management responsibilities, and less casework.

Once you have your basic social work qualification, you can go on to study for post-qualifying awards in specialist areas of work, such as family therapy or childcare law.

Adults: note that there is no upper age limit for entry on to DipSW courses, and mature candidates are usually welcomed.

SOCIAL WORK
IN THE HEALTH SERVICE

Hospital patients, or people having to cope with medical problems in their own homes, often have to face extra financial and family difficulties caused by their illness. For this reason, some social workers specialise in working in or with hospitals, clinics and GP practices. You need a good education to begin training as a social worker.

What the work involves

Many of the cases dealt with will be similar to those in the community at large, such as finding childcare provision when a parent is in hospital, or helping an elderly person cope at home after a serious illness. Often, helping patients to solve their domestic and financial problems can play an important part in their recovery.

A lot of the openings involve work with psychiatric patients and their families, but there are also opportunities with general hospitals and special medical units. Specialist social workers are particularly required where long-term care of the patient is involved, and where medical problems have a particularly close connection with social problems – psychiatric disturbance, drug and alcohol dependence, cases of criminal conviction, etc. There is also a need for specialist social workers to work as liaison officers between the health team (doctors, nurses, etc) and the social services department.

Medical social workers are employed by the local authority social services department. They may be based in a hospital, or in a local authority department, or they may have a responsibility which is split between the two. A job may combine special health service work with normal casework.

GETTING STARTED

Wherever the medical social worker is based, it is necessary to have undergone exactly the same general training as other social workers. It is also necessary for the would-be medical social worker to be prepared to gain experience of general casework before specialising. It may be necessary to take an ordinary social work job when specialist posts (which are often senior positions) are not available. Anyone interested in health service social work therefore needs to obtain general information on the job of social worker and how to train for it.

Adults

As with all social work careers, mature entrants are especially welcome: adults may be admitted to social work training with qualifications lower than those expected of younger applicants, though they will still need to prove they can cope with a demanding training course. The Central Council for Education and Training in Social Work (CCETSW) can give information and advice to anyone interested in this kind of career.

THE PROBATION SERVICE

The probation service, like the courts and the prison service, is part of the judicial system, and its work is backed up by the law. It has a supervisory role, representing the authority of the court, and at the same time it offers guidance and support to help offenders to redirect their lives. Professional training is given to people with relevant experience and qualifications.

What it takes

This might be a suitable job for you if:

- you are mature and well balanced;
- you can form relationships with people from all walks of life;
- you can gain people's trust, and yet be authoritative when necessary;
- you can work in the formal setting of a law court, and in prisons and youth custody centres;
- you are prepared to take a demanding training course;
- you are prepared to do a lot of report-writing for courts and prison parole boards;
- you are willing to work in the evenings and at weekends;
- you can drive and are willing to do a lot of travelling.

Working with people

Contrary to popular belief, most of the probation officer's work is not with young people, but with adults. They also work closely with other agencies, such as local authority social services departments, the Department of Social Security and voluntary bodies.

Probation officers need to be able to form personal relationships with offenders and others, many of whom may be very hostile and uncooperative. They must win trust, and yet be able also to exercise the authority of the legal system which they represent. It can be difficult to get this balance right.

Court orders and community work

Probation officers are concerned with offenders who are subject to court orders of various kinds. They supervise offenders who have been placed under a probation order, for a fixed period of time, by the courts. They also supervise community service projects and day centres. They can be involved in victim support, sometimes mediating between offenders and their victims. They also try to provide 'preventive' care – encouraging interests and activities such as community work and outdoor pursuits, which may help to prevent offenders from getting into further trouble by giving them a sense of purpose and of belonging.

In prison and after . . .

With prisoners in detention, the probation officer's job is to help and advise them in all sorts of ways: sorting out family and marriage problems, and advising young offenders on education and training. A probation officer who works in a prison or other detention centre may be known as a **prison welfare officer**.

When prisoners leave custody, a probation officer will be involved in aftercare. In close liaison with the prison welfare officer, probation officers supervise prisoners on parole, help ex-prisoners to find work and housing and to understand the benefits system, or find rehabilitation centres for those who have spent many years in prison and become 'institutionalised'.

Not just offenders

Although work with offenders is its major task, the probation service also deals with custody recommendations, and

arrangements for access where children are involved in divorce cases. This area of work calls for a high degree of tact and sensitivity.

GETTING STARTED

In the past, probation officers have been qualified social workers. New regulations mean that this is no longer the case, although people who qualified as social workers – with or without Home Office sponsorship – before 1997 are exempt from the need for further professional training.

The new arrangements are intended to encourage a wider range of mature candidates to apply for training, as attendance on a full-time diploma course is not required. Area probation services will recruit people directly as salaried trainees; there will be no centralised Home Office sponsorship scheme.

Training and assessment will be mostly in the workplace, but with an additional input from higher education institutions, as a considerable amount of background knowledge is required as well as skills and work experience. Previous qualifications and experience – such as police work, social work or community work – will be taken into account, and may allow exemptions from some of the training modules. Diplomas in Social Work with options in criminal justice and youth justice are still on offer, but it is unclear how much exemption they will qualify for.

Successful trainees will be granted Qualified Probation Officer Status (QPOS), backed up by an NVQ at an appropriate level.

COUNSELLING CAREERS

When people feel they have a problem or are unhappy with some aspect of their lives, they might seek the help of a counsellor. That problem may involve experiencing distress, having a difficult decision to make, or a crisis to face. In private, and in confidence, counsellors help people to clarify and understand their problems, and find ways of meeting, or addressing, their needs.

What is counselling?

It is much easier to say what counselling is *not*, than to say what it *is*. It does not mean sitting in judgment on other people, or persuading them to follow a particular course of action, or giving advice (*'If I were you . . .'*). Counselling takes place through a two-way relationship between the counsellor and the client. The counsellor helps clients to talk about their problem, getting to the root of it by listening to what they say, and asking questions which may probe deeper into certain issues relating to the problem. This will enable clients to learn about themselves, to assist them to find ways of getting to grips with the problem, and to grow and change as human beings.

Perhaps the client is a child who is very unhappy at home, and not doing well at school – or a woman who feels she can no longer communicate with her husband. Perhaps it's someone with an alcohol problem, or a teenage girl who is pregnant and under pressure from her family to have an abortion. Maybe it's someone who, since being made redundant, feels depressed and useless, or a student who is unable to cope with the pressure of exams.

Where do counsellors work?

Counsellors work in a variety of settings, including schools, colleges, universities, etc, as well as special services or agencies set up to deal with specific types of problems. Full-time jobs for counsellors tend to be in educational settings, in workplace staff-counselling services and within the National Health Service. Other opportunities, especially outside large cities, are more likely to be part-time or voluntary activities.

Counsellors may work with their clients on the whole range of problems which they present. On the other hand, they may decide to refer a client to a more specialised source of help if that seems appropriate. Some counsellors become specialists in particular types of problem – e.g. in marriage guidance, bereavement, AIDS, drugs or alcohol-abuse counselling – or with a certain age range, especially teenagers and young adults.

There are many other professions where counselling skills and training are relevant. These include youth work, careers guidance, social work, church work, psychology, psychiatry and many aspects of medicine. There are also wide opportunities in voluntary work – with organisations such as RELATE (previously the Marriage Guidance Council), Cruse for bereavement care, or special counselling services for young people, adult relatives of alcoholics, AIDS sufferers, drug users, etc.

What it takes

A counsellor is someone who:

- readily establishes a good relationship with people;
- is capable of listening carefully, interpreting what the person is saying accurately and sensitively;
- can, on occasions, infer what a person is *not* saying;
- is able to gain the complete trust of a client;

- is patient and tolerant and does not pass judgement or offer personal advice;
- is in touch with the client, understanding and seeing things from the client's point of view;
- is a sensitive and stable person;
- has a high level of self-awareness, knowing what personal resources to offer the client.

Counselling is not a career for a very young person. Considerable maturity is needed and, while some younger people might use counselling skills in their particular profession, it would be very unusual for people to enter full-time counselling work before their mid-twenties; many are considerably older.

TRAINING

Because counselling is a 'second' career, people wishing to work in counselling will almost always first gain professional qualifications and experience in a related area of work. The most obviously related occupational areas are teaching, careers advisory work, psychology, psychotherapy, youth and community work, the creative therapies such as drama therapy and art therapy, church work and social/probation work. Medical and health professions also give rise to opportunities for counselling. Many people enter counselling after working in the voluntary sector.

There is a broad range of training available in counselling, with a mixture of long, short, full-time and part-time courses being offered. Some courses are geared towards a particular type of counselling role – e.g. educational counselling, church work, careers guidance, bereavement help or marriage guidance.

Courses are offered by many types of providers, including universities, local colleges of further education, private training organisations and bodies such as RELATE and the National

Childbirth Trust. People wishing to work as school counsellors will almost certainly be expected to be qualified teachers with substantial teaching experience.

COURSES

There are full-time and part-time masters' degrees (such as MEd and MA) and certificate/diploma courses in guidance, counselling and related subjects. These are 'long' courses for professionally qualified people such as teachers, psychologists and church workers.

Also, there are various short courses (ranging from a few days to a term or more), both full-time and part-time, in aspects of counselling.

Some short courses have specific entry requirements – such as qualified teacher status; others are more flexible and may be suitable for voluntary workers. Some courses are geared very specifically to the needs of the organisations running them – e.g. RELATE or specific young persons' counselling services. It would be worth contacting your local college of further education to see what kind of short courses are on offer: there may well be something, at least at an introductory level.

Accreditation by the British Association for Counselling (BAC) requires evidence of counselling practice and supervision by an experienced counsellor, so practical experience in counselling work must accompany theoretical training.

CAREERS WITH SOCIOLOGY

Sociology is one of the major social sciences. It is the study of the behaviour of people, and the relationships between them, within social groups. Sociologists study how individuals' needs and wants vary according to the social group to which they belong. Sociologists have degrees.

Sociologists study, research and analyse how society works, in a systematic way. The kind of issues that interest sociologists are:

- the effects of changes in work and technology;
- causes of increases in certain types of crime;
- changes in family life in recent years;
- how people's health relates to their role in society;
- the role of religion in modern society.

Studying sociology

Sociology is offered at GCSE or A level in many schools and colleges. Beyond that, it can be studied as a degree subject at universities and colleges of higher education, either on its own or in combination with one or more other subjects.

If you have a serious interest in sociology, and perhaps in working as a sociologist, then a degree is necessary. You don't have to have taken GCSE or A level in sociology to be able to apply for a degree course – in fact, many students studying sociology in higher education have had no previous experience of the subject beyond general interest reading. What you will normally need is a minimum of two A levels, a BTEC National Diploma or Advanced GNVQ, plus supporting GCSEs. Some institutions require you to have GCSE maths and/or English at grade C – check carefully. Adults may well find that entry requirements can be relaxed for them.

EDUCATION AND TRAINING IN SOCIOLOGY

The starting point is to take a degree course at a university or college of higher education. Courses range from single honours sociology to joint courses where sociology can be studied alongside other social science subjects, arts subjects, a modern language, etc. *Which Degree?* and the CRAC *Degree Course Guide* give more information on courses.

Careers for sociology graduates
Working as a sociologist

Sociologists are required in the field of research and are to be found in the Civil Service, local authorities, research bodies and commissions, and universities and other types of higher education. The government, at both local and national level, uses sociologists to look at the possible effects of new legislation and the results of past government activities, in such areas as education, health, social welfare, employment and leisure activities. Research of all types is also carried out by other bodies, such as the Equal Opportunities Commission, the Commission for Racial Equality, and various projects based at universities. Research jobs go only to highly qualified sociologists – those with a good BA, BSc or BSocSci degree, followed by a higher degree.

Teaching

There are some opportunities to teach in higher education (universities and colleges of HE) for well-qualified sociologists. In higher education, sociology is taught to undergraduates specialising in sociology and other social sciences, and to students training to work in medicine, education, housing management, etc. Sociology also forms a part of general or liberal studies programmes. Lecturers in higher education institutions, particularly universities, normally undertake research work of their own alongside their teaching commitments.

Sociology is also taught in colleges and schools, often to GCSE and A level. However, in schools, you would usually teach another subject as well, or work part-time, as a full timetable of sociology would be unlikely. You should note that sociology is not at present recommended as a single-honours degree subject

for intending teachers (despite its obvious relevance to gaining an understanding of children): official advice is to study at least 50 per cent of your degree in a subject which is itself a main school curriculum subject, such as English, mathematics or history. You might therefore wish to consider a joint degree in sociology and another subject, if you want to study sociology without jeopardising a possible career in teaching.

Social work

Compared with graduates of other subjects, a high proportion of sociology graduates go into jobs related to social and welfare work. This is not surprising, given their interest in people. But, on its own, a sociology degree does not provide training for social work. If you want to become a social worker, you need to take a further professional training course lasting two years, with some exceptions depending on the course content of the particular sociology degree you have taken (see earlier section). If you know in advance that you want a career in social work, you might want to consider applying for one of the degree courses which combines the study of sociology with the opportunity to also gain a professional qualification (DipSW).

Other opportunities

Sociology graduates go into a wide range of jobs, and it is sensible to think of a sociology degree as giving you an opening into general graduate-level employment, rather than as being a vocational subject. Besides social and welfare work, over a third of graduates take up careers in business management, marketing or finance. Sociology graduates certainly have plenty of scope when it comes to careers, and there is no need to make up your mind too early about what you will eventually do.

CAREERS WITH PSYCHOLOGY

Psychologists study what people and animals do, and investigate, by scientific means, *why* they do it. They use their understanding of behaviour to help solve people's problems and worries, and to improve the quality of their lives. To become a psychologist, you need a degree.

Psychologists investigate such things as:

- how children learn to speak their language;
- how humans and animals learn new skills;
- what motivates humans and animals to acquire new skills;
- why people, including close relatives, have different personalities;
- how people 'get on' with each other – how they interact;
- how drugs, such as alcohol and psychiatric drugs, affect behaviour;
- how people behave in groups and crowds.

Psychology must not be confused with *psychiatry*, which is a branch of medicine practised by qualified doctors who are specialists in disorders which affect the mind. Psychologists do not undergo medical training.

Where psychologists work, and what they do

The British Psychological Society has a membership of about 22,000, including student members. Central government is one of the largest individual employers, with a staff of over 250 psychologists. Many psychologists, including educational psychologists, are employed by local authorities. More are employed as clinical psychologists, mostly in the National Health Service.

Clinical psychologist

Clinical psychologists work in the health services – in psychiatric and general hospitals, in out-patients' clinics, community health centres and some social services departments. They deal with behavioural problems and abnormalities, including stress, anxiety and depression, treating clients through counselling and behaviour therapy. Tests and other assessment methods are used to gain information about clients' intelligence, interests and personalities. Clinical psychologists are involved in the care and assisting of people with learning difficulties, and they liaise closely with other members of the health team, including doctors, nurses and occupational therapists.

Clinical psychologists should not be confused with psychiatrists, who are qualified doctors, specialising in psychiatric medicine, who employ drugs, surgery and, sometimes, electrical treatment to alleviate patients' conditions.

Educational psychologist

Educational psychologists are concerned with the psychological and educational development of children and young people in the home, at school and in the community. They investigate learning, behaviour and emotional difficulties in children and young people, and advise teachers, parents and others on ways of helping their clients. Posts are usually located in the psychological services department of a local educational authority. Educational psychologists contribute to the work of other organisations, such as child guidance clinics and social service observation and assessment centres.

Occupational psychologist

Occupational psychologists work in government and industry, where they are concerned with many aspects of occupational behaviour. An occupational psychologist is an expert in matters such as vocational assessment and guidance, job performance, job satisfaction and motivation.

A psychologist could be involved in advising on, or participating in, the way in which a firm selects its employees.

Occupational psychologists devise aptitude and personality tests to see if applicants are suitable, and may interview them. Occupational psychologists could also be involved in advising on the training needs of employees, and finding ways of getting the best performance out of individual employees. Their work is often closely linked with that of personnel and training officers.

Some occupational psychologists specialise in vocational guidance and problems of career choice, but it is not necessary to be a psychologist in order to undertake this sort of work.

Forensic psychologist

Psychology graduates are employed in various Home Office establishments, including youth treatment centres, remand centres, special hospitals and prisons, working closely with other prison staff in the assessment and treatment of prisoners. They are involved in staff training, and the psychological aspects of organisation of the prison system. Forensic psychologists also work with police, lawyers and court officials.

Dennis – forensic psychologist

‘ When I informed my family that I was to start work as an forensic psychologist, they felt it would be challenging and exciting, but would be glad to see me return home after my first day!

First impressions were alien – I had to get accustomed to fences, different locks with different keys, uniforms, rules and the general pattern of existence in a closed establishment.

Now, the prison confines have become a commonplace background, against which I deal with correspondence, interview individual prisoners (they are real people, after all!) often with a view to writing reports for the Mental Health Review Tribunal, or attempting psychotherapeutic work with aggressive or anxious individuals.

I run workshops for the nursing staff of the attached hospital, and for other groups of workers, on subjects such as: dealing with violence through non-violent means, or anger management with potentially violent prisoners. The work involves a considerable amount of training – for me, in the early stages. Now, I train volunteer prison workers in the teaching of social skills, as well as training individual prisoners myself.

After some years of experience in this branch of psychology, I was invited to lecture to postgraduates at our local university psychology department on very specific topics, for example on dangerousness, or on the prediction of disturbance in an institution and possible methods of its prevention.

As with any professional-level job, there is a lot of administration and paperwork to get through each week, and the work can be hard and sometimes tiring, but I have gained confidence in my own competence. It's a long time since that daunting solo interview with my first prisoner!

Teaching psychology

Psychology is taught as an A level or GCSE subject in some schools and colleges, and as a degree subject in universities. Aspects of psychology are also taught as a part of many professional training courses and degree-level studies in related subjects. For example, trainee teachers study child psychology and the psychology of interpersonal behaviour; social science students take courses in social psychology; careers advisers learn about the psychology of adolescence and techniques of assessing abilities, interests and personality.

There are, therefore, opportunities for teaching psychology in a wide range of institutions: universities, colleges of further and higher education, schools and adult education centres. In universities and colleges of higher education, a psychology lecturer may well undertake research as well as teaching.

Community, social and child psychology

Psychologists can be employed to investigate many different situations. They may look at possible causes of vandalism, say, or reasons for differences in child-rearing amongst families from different social classes. They may try to sort out the problems encountered by people living in institutions such as orphanages or long-stay hospitals. Psychologists investigating problems like these might be employed as part of a project team, which includes sociologists and educationists. The range of possibilities in this field is wide.

Research psychology

Research units are found in academic institutions, industry and government departments. Research psychologists need to know about methods of experimental design, investigative techniques and statistical methods. They investigate all sorts of problems, including those mentioned earlier.

Other opportunities

A knowledge of psychology could be a valuable basis for a career in many fields, including social work, advertising and market research, personnel work, police work, journalism, careers advisory work and the probation service. Specialised training for these occupations could be undertaken after obtaining a degree – see the relevant sections in this book. Probably, less than a quarter of psychology graduates are employed as psychologists.

HOW TO BECOME A PSYCHOLOGIST

The normal first step towards a career as a professional psychologist is to take an honours degree in psychology (BA or BSc). Courses are offered by almost all universities, including, on a part-time basis, the Open University, and by some colleges. Ensure that the degree course which you choose to follow has been approved by the British Psychological Society, for later registration as a Chartered Psychologist following postgraduate professional training. If you take a degree course in a different subject, it is possible to obtain membership of the British Psychological Society by taking a one-year full-time, or two-year part-time, conversion course, or by taking the Society's Qualifying Examination.

Psychology graduates who go on to take postgraduate training in a specific area of psychology are entitled to register with the British Psychological Society as **chartered psychologists**. Qualification as a Chartered Psychologist is becoming an essential requirement for many posts in psychology.

Qualifications needed for a degree course in psychology
At least two A levels, but preferably three, are required. Universities are likely to ask for high A level grades. Subject requirements vary from place to place: suitable A level subjects include mathematics and biology, but arts and social science subjects are also appropriate. A level psychology is not required.

Most courses require GCSE at grade C in mathematics. Some courses require GCSEs in double science at grade C. AS levels/Advanced GNVQ/BTEC National Diploma may be accepted as alternative entry qualifications. You should check the requirements of individual courses on the ECCTIS database,

107

in higher education handbooks, or with the prospectuses of individual establishments.

TRAINING FOR PARTICULAR BRANCHES OF PSYCHOLOGY

Clinical psychologist
A first requirement is a degree, recognised by the British Psychological Society, followed by either a two- or three-year postgraduate course at a university, or a three-year period working as a probationer, receiving in-service training leading to an MSc in Clinical Psychology. Once qualified, the trainee is appointed as a grade A clinical psychologist.

Educational psychologist
Educational psychologists are trained both as psychologists and as teachers. The normal method of training consists of four steps:

- an honours degree in psychology, which is recognised by the BPS. A second class honours standard is the accepted minimum. This takes three years;
- Postgraduate Certificate in Education (PGCE) – one year;
- at least two years' teaching experience;
- postgraduate training in educational psychology – usually one year, leading to a Master's degree.

These steps can be followed in the order given. Alternatively, qualified teachers can take a psychology degree part-time – e.g. through the Open University – and then go on to the special postgraduate course. Another route for non-psychology graduates is to take a one-year full-time conversion course in psychology, available at one or two higher education establishments, but obtaining a grant could be difficult.

Occupational psychologist

This requires a degree in psychology, and an approved post-graduate training course, or the British Psychological Society's Postgraduate Certificate in Occupational Psychology. Appropriate supervised experience is also required.

Research psychology

A good honours degree is required (of first, or upper second class standard) followed by a higher degree (MSc or PhD).

Forensic psychologist

Jobs may be found in the Prison Service and the NHS. In-service training for chartered psychologists is the only training route at present.

Related occupations

Although quite a different occupation, there are some aspects of psychology which overlap with **psychotherapy.** Psychotherapy is aimed at helping people to understand the causes of their distress and to come to terms with their problems. The emphasis is on verbal communication. To become a psychotherapist, you need a degree, followed by at least four years' training. Hypnosis is used as an aid to recall, in some forms of psychotherapy.

CREATIVE THERAPIES

The creative therapies include opportunities for specialists in dance, drama, music and art. Qualified therapists can work in a variety of settings – such as hospitals, clinics, special schools and prisons – helping patients to express themselves and communicate.

What are creative therapies?

Creative activities have a useful role as a form of therapy or treatment for people who have difficulty in expressing themselves, or who need a stimulus to help them take part in activities. Psychiatric patients, children with emotional difficulties or people with learning difficulties can sometimes only communicate freely through art, drama or music. Other patients, with medical problems, may benefit from the exercise of painting, playing a musical instrument, or taking part in drama, dance or other artistic expression.

Posts in the creative therapies are rather scarce and not highly paid, with part-time and sessional work being more usual than full-time posts. Many therapists carry out their work within an existing job, such as nursing, teaching, psychology or occupational therapy.

What it takes

All creative therapy involves very demanding work, especially where psychiatric or emotionally disturbed patients are concerned. The therapist must develop a relationship with patients which will help them to express their feelings through the medium being used. The strength of feelings shown can make the therapist feel very involved with patients, making it difficult to leave the working day behind.

Because it requires great sensitivity and maturity, working in creative therapy is really a career for experienced adults, rather than for young school- or college-leavers. Young people should start by getting training in the particular art form they want to use.

Art therapy

Art therapists often work with emotionally disturbed or non-communicative patients, in child guidance clinics or psychiatric units. They try to develop a close relationship with patients which will help them express themselves and come to a better understanding of themselves. A patient's work can be kept as a record of development which can be referred to by the patient, therapist or other colleagues at any time.

Art therapists work in both private and local authority special schools, guidance and psychotherapy clinics, psychiatric hospitals, occupational therapy departments of hospitals, units for disturbed adolescents, prisons, etc.

TRAINING

Training is open to graduates in art or design or qualified professionals such as teachers or therapists who have artistic ability. Mature, flexible people are needed, with at least a year's experience of work in the health service, education or community.

Music therapy

Music therapy mainly involves work with adults and children suffering from physical, mental or emotional difficulties, rather than physical illnesses, though there are some opportunities with elderly people, in hospices, and with prisoners. The therapist is likely to work not only with individuals but also with groups. Posts are available with education authorities, independent special schools, social services departments, prisons and hospitals. Therapists may be employed full-time, part-time, or on a sessional basis.

TRAINING

The first step is normally to gain qualifications in music (degree or diploma) and then take one of the music therapy courses approved by the British Society of Music Therapy (see Further Information section). There may be openings for people with other professional qualifications, such as psychology, general or special needs teaching, etc, but you would still need a high level of musicianship (gained through spare-time activities, for instance). Note that if you want to work in local education authority schools as a music therapist, you will usually need to have a teaching qualification.

Dance therapy

As with the other creative therapies, the work is mainly with adults and children with learning difficulties, psychiatrically ill patients, and elderly people, either in the community or as part of a team in a hospital. Therapists also work in the community with other groups, such as youth clubs and schools.

The Association of Dance Therapists (International) has set up a range of training courses (mainly by distance learning, supported by optional practical workshops) – see the Further Information section. Those who have studied with the Association so far include nurses, physiotherapists, occupational and recreational therapists, psychologists, dance teachers and dance students. Holders of the Association's Diploma can do supervised voluntary work in hospitals, if they are not in a job which enables them to get experience.

TRAINING

There are degree courses, postgraduate qualifications and private courses available in dance therapy. There are also relevant full- and part-time courses in eurythmy, offered in association with the Rudolf Steiner Organisation.

Dramatherapy

Dramatherapy is a technique usually used with groups rather than individuals. A dramatherapist might work with a group of disturbed adolescents, a group of prisoners or psychiatric patients, or with physically and mentally disabled people of all ages. Dramatherapy is also used with people who are not ill or seriously disturbed at all, but who want help in learning to express their emotions.

The aims of dramatherapy can be very wide-ranging. The therapist working with people with physical and/or mental

disabilities might be trying to get them moving better, improving their balance and their speech, perhaps improving basic social and life skills. Role-play is often used to help patients express emotions such as anger and fear.

Rather than being a full-time profession, dramatherapy is often used by people already working in the health services (e.g. clinical psychologists, mental health nurses), education, psychotherapy or other counselling roles.

TRAINING

There are various postgraduate training courses in dramatherapy, intended for people already using dramatherapy in their work, and they include theoretical and workshop study, as well as supervised work experience.

Horticultural therapy

The use of horticulture as a therapy technique for people with special needs is well established. Opportunities occur in centres run by social services departments, hospitals, sheltered workshops and specialist colleges. (See *Horticulture, Forestry & Farming* in the *Just the Job!* series for details on how to train as a horticulturist.)

RELIGIOUS WORH

Churches and religious organisations recruit adults with a wide experience of life and a true vocation to the service of the particular religion and the community. Each religious organisation has its own 'structure' of leadership and lay-workers. You are likely to know how all this functions within your own faith – or you can find out from your own local religious representative.

Churches and religious organisations do not offer employment as ministers or leaders to school-leavers, who obviously do not have enough maturity or experience of life for such a demanding job. They may, of course, have occasional jobs in areas like administration, secretarial work, publicity and communications. Most religions are very keen to encourage young people to involve themselves in religious activities and to offer themselves for service when they are older. There are generally plenty of opportunities to get involved with Sunday Schools (or equivalents), youth clubs, old people's clubs, etc.

GETTING STARTED

Young people who think they may be interested in a church career are generally advised to continue their education to degree level (in theology or another discipline), or to take a course of training (e.g. nursing, teaching or social work) which will be useful to them in religious service later on. Adults too may wish to pursue theological studies as a preparation for their vocation – but seek advice from your own church or faith before embarking on any course of action. Voluntary social work – either in this country or abroad – can also provide very useful experience to adults and young people alike.

The minimum age to be considered for church work is normally eighteen, but it is often desirable to delay application until at least the second year of a degree or professional training course, as there is a strong preference for more mature applicants.

Some useful addresses – for Christian and non-Christian faiths – are given in the Further Information section, but the list is by no means inclusive.

Opportunities

Most entrants to religious work of whatever denomination work in the British Isles, rather than abroad. They may be part of a group or team ministry, working within a local community and ministering to the needs of local people, with each member of the team contributing their own particular gifts to the work, or they may work on their own.

Other opportunities exist in specialisms such as **chaplaincies** to hospitals, prisons, universities and schools, to industry and to the Forces. Some people may choose to become members of a religious community. Christian churches overseas also welcome men and women for missionary work. They need not only ordained clergy, but also lay Christians who are able to offer a wide variety of skills, and teachers, medical workers, agriculturalists, youth workers, accountants and many other professionally trained people are welcomed.

Some opportunities for religious work may be restricted by gender and/or marital status, and paid employment within minority religions in the UK is likely to be limited.

JOBS WITH CHARITIES

Whilst by far the largest part of charity work is done by unpaid helpers, charities and voluntary organisations themselves employ many people in both part-time and full-time work. These people may help those in need by raising and administering funds, doing research work, encouraging others to help themselves, or they may work as advisers or carers. There are salaried positions for mature adults who have gained paid or voluntary experience.

Some salaries and wages paid by voluntary organisations are low. However, the larger organisations now offer good pay to attract more highly skilled people, who can cut costs in other ways and raise funds more effectively. Jobs are mostly the same as those found in the public or commercial sectors. They include:

Publicity, advertising and fundraising
Decisions have to be made about the best ways of getting the charity's message across to the public so that there is money to be used. A charity has to raise funds, and then spend the money in the best way it can. The Institute of Charity Fundraising Managers offers short courses in fundraising techniques.

Financial control
Some charities, like Oxfam and Save the Children, are large organisations with annual budgets of millions of pounds; others are quite small and specialised. Whatever the size, it is no good having a charity which spends all its money on administration, with nothing getting through to those who need it.

Retailing

Some charities run chains of shops, such as the familiar Help the Aged, Sue Ryder and Oxfam shops. Some retailers offer specially manufactured Third World products, as well as second-hand items. Running a chain of shops like this requires people with retailing and accounting skills.

Management

Large organisations need people with management skills to look after the staff, and to make sure that everything runs smoothly. They are often looking for people who have a proven track record in the voluntary work sector, or who bring transferable skills from another sector.

Types of organisations

Voluntary organisations can be divided into four categories:

Those providing services directly to people in need – such as Barnardo's, Help the Aged, NSPCC and the Cyrenians. This is where the majority of the paid work is found – most commonly for social and care workers, nurses, paramedics, teachers, advice workers, managers and administrators, clerical and secretarial staff, fund-raisers, public relations officers and information workers.

Those whose main function is research and publicity – such as the Child Poverty Action Group, Liberty and the various organisations researching into specific diseases. There are opportunities for researchers, administrators, clerical staff, public relations personnel, etc.

Those who mainly encourage self-help and community action – such as the Pre-school Learning Alliance, Mind and the National Schizophrenia Fellowship. These mainly employ administrators, but some community workers too.

Those which aim to increase the effectiveness of voluntary bodies – such as the National Council for Voluntary Organisations, National Association of Citizens' Advice Bureaux, The Volunteer Centre UK. Again, these associations have administrative, information and publicity posts.

See the Further Information section for further sources and some useful addresses.

FOR FURTHER INFORMATION

WORKING WITH CHILDREN

Association of Nursery Training Colleges – The Princess Christian College, 26 Wilbraham Road, Fallowfield, Manchester M14 6JX. Tel: 0161 224 4560.

CACHE (Council for Awards in Children's Care and Education) – 8 Chequer Street, St Albans, Hertfordshire AL1 3XZ. Tel: 01727 847636. Provides details on the CACHE courses. Please send a stamped addressed envelope.

HAPA – Adventure Play for Children with Disabilities and Special Needs – Pryor's Bank, Bishop's Park, London SW6 3LA. Tel: 0171 731 1435.

Kids Club Network – Bellerive House, 3 Muirfield Crescent, London E14 9SZ. Tel: 0171 512 2112. Offers training programmes for developing skills in playwork, and is developing a careers pack for interested individuals wanting to enter work in the playcare field.

NAMCW – The National Association for Maternal and Child Welfare Ltd – First Floor, 40–42 Osnaburgh Street, London NW1 3ND. Tel: 0171 383 4541.

National Association of Nursery Nurses – 12 The Wayside, Hurworth on Tees, Darlington, Co. Durham DL2 2EE. Tel: 01325 720511.

National Childminding Association – 8 Masons Hill, Bromley, Kent BR2 9EY. Tel: 0181 464 6164. Produces a range of publications giving advice on all aspects of childminding.

National Foster Care Association – Leonard House, 5–7 Marshalsea Road, London SE1 1EP. Tel: 0171 828 6266. Issues free information pack on fostering.

National Play Information Centre – 199 Knightsbridge, London SW7 1DE. Tel: 0171 584 6464.

NCH Action for Children – 85 Highbury Park, London N5 1UD. Tel: 0171 226 2033.

Play–Train – 31 Farm Road, Birmingham B11 1LS. Tel: 0121 766 8446.

Playlink – The Co-op Centre, Unit 5, 11 Mowll Street, London SW9 6BG. Tel: 0171 820 3800.

Pre-School Learning Alliance – 69 Kings Cross Road, London WC1X 9LL. Tel: 0171 833 0991.

Professional Association of Nursery Nurses – 2 St James's Court, Friar Gate, Derby DE1 1BT. Tel: 01332 343029 – provides leaflets giving guidelines for nannies; advice on setting up a day nursery, etc.

Spirito – (The Specialist Industry Training Organisation for Sport, Recreation, Playwork, Outdoor Education & Development Training), Euston House, 81–103 Euston Street, London NW1 2ET. Tel: 0171 388 3111.

Careers Working with Children and Young People, published by Kogan Page.

Working in Work with Children, published by COIC.

YOUTH WORK

National Youth Agency – 17–23 Albion Street, Leicester LE1 6GD. Tel: 0116 285 6789.

Youth Clubs UK – 11 St Bride Street, London EC4A 4AS. Tel: 0171 353 2366.

YMCA – 640 Forest Road, Walthamstow, London E17 3DZ. Tel: 0181 520 5599.

YWCA – Clarendon House, 52 Cornmarket Street, Oxford OX1 3EJ. Tel: 01865 726110.

The NYA Guide to Initial Training Courses in Youth and Community Work is available from the National Youth Agency (address above).

NYA Guide to Becoming a Youth Worker is also obtainable from the National Youth Agency.

CAREERS ADVISORY WORK

College of Guidance Studies – College Road, Hextable, Swanley, Kent BR8 7RN. Tel: 01322 664407.

Institute of Careers Guidance – 27a Lower High Street, Stourbridge, West Midlands DY8 1TA. Tel: 01384 376464 – services include providing vacancy information covering a wide range of opportunities in careers guidance.

Local Government Management Board – Arndale House, The Arndale Centre, Luton, Bedfordshire LU1 2TS. Tel: 01582 451166 – for further details of careers service work, and of courses leading to the Dip CG and of centres accrediting NVQs.

WORKING WITH ELDERLY PEOPLE

Age Concern England – Astral House, 1268 London Road SW16 4ER. Tel: 0181 679 8000.

Central Council for Education and Training in Social Work (CCETSW) – Derbyshire House, St. Chad's Street, London WC1H 8AD. Tel: 0171 278 2455.

Central Council for Education and Training in Social Work (CCETSW) Cymru – Information Service, 2nd Floor, West Wing, South Gate House, Wood Street, Cardiff CF1 1EW. Tel: 01222 226257.

Help the Aged – Information Department, St James's Walk, London EC1R 0BE. Tel: 0171 253 0253. Can provide a useful booklet *Giving Good Care*.

WORKING WITH PEOPLE WITH SPECIAL NEEDS

Camphill Rudolph Steiner Schools – Central Office, Murtle Estate, Bieldside, Aberdeen AB15 9EP. Tel: 01224 867935.

Camphill Village Trust – Delrow House, Hillfield Lane, Aldenham, Watford, Hertfordshire WD2 8DJ. Tel: 01923 856006.

City Lit Centre for Deaf People – Keeley House, Keeley Street, London WC2B 4BA. Tel: 0171 430 0548.

Henshaw's College – Bogs Lane, Starbeck, Harrogate, North Yorkshire HG1 4ED. Tel: 01423 886451.

Royal National Institute for the Blind (RNIB) – 224 Great Portland Street, London W1N 6AA. Tel: 0171 388 1266.

School of Social Work and RNIB Rehabilitation Studies – Faculty of Health and Community Care, University of Central England, Perry Barr, Birmingham B42 2SU. Tel: 0121 331 6405.

SOCIAL AND PROBATION WORK

Barnardo's – Tanners Lane, Barkingside, Ilford, Essex IG6 1QG. Tel: 0181 550 8822.

Central Council for Education and Training in Social Work (CCETSW) – Derbyshire House, St. Chad's Street, London WC1H 8AD. Tel: 0171 278 2455.

Central Council for Education and Training in Social Work (CCETSW) Wales – Information Service, 2nd Floor, West Wing, South Gate House, Wood Street, Cardiff CF1 1EW. Tel: 01222 226257.

The Children's Society – Edward Rudolf House, Margery Street, London WC1X 0JL. Tel: 0171 837 4299.

NCH Action for Children – 85 Highbury Park, London N5 1UD. Tel: 0171 226 2033.

National Association of Probation Officers (NAPO) – 4 Chivalry Road, London SW11 1HT. Tel: 0171 223 4887.

Probation Service Division – C6 Division, Home Office, 50 Queen Anne's Gate, London SW1H 9AT. Tel: 0171 273 2675.

Working in Social Work, published by COIC.

Social Work and Probation Work, an AGCAS booklet for graduates, available from CSU, Armstrong House, Oxford Road, Manchester M1 7ED. Tel: 0161 236 9816, ext 250/251.

COUNSELLING

British Association for Counselling – 1 Regent Place, Rugby, Warwickshire CV21 2PJ. Information line: 01788 578328. A free information booklet on counselling and available training can be sent on receipt of an A4 stamped, addressed envelope. BAC publishes a range of information on counselling, most of it priced. A complete publications catalogue can be sent on receipt of a stamped, addressed envelope.

SOCIOLOGY

British Sociological Association – Unit 3G, Mountjoy Research Centre, Stockton Road, Durham DH1 3UR. Tel: 0191 383 0839. Produces the leaflet *Sociology: information and opportunities*.

PSYCHOLOGY

Association of Child Psychotherapists – 120 West Heath Road, London NW3 7TU. Tel: 0181 458 1609.

Association of Educational Psychologists – 3 Sunderland Road, Gilesgate, Durham DH1 2LH. Tel: 0191 384 9512.

British Confederation of Psychotherapy – 37A Mapesbury Road, London NW2 4HJ. Tel: 0181 830 5173. Can provide information about training in psychotherapy.

British Psychological Society – St Andrew's House, 48 Princess Road East, Leicester LE1 7DR. Tel: 0116 254 9568. Publishes a range of booklets and books concerning training and careers using psychology, such as *Putting Psychology to Work* and *Career Choices in Psychology*.

UK Council for Psychotherapy – First Floor, 167–169 Great Portland Street, London W1N 5FB. Tel: 0171 436 3002.

Which Psychology Degree Course?, by Anthony Gale, published by the British Psychological Society.

The CRAC *Degree Course Guide: Psychology* provides a useful introduction to the various courses available.

CREATIVE THERAPIES

Association of Dance Therapists (International) – 19 Ashlake Road, Streatham, London SW16 2BB. Tel/fax: 0181 677 5624.

British Association of Art Therapists – 11a Richmond Road, Brighton, Sussex BN2 3RL.

British Association for Dramatherapists – 41 Broomhouse Lane, Hurlingham Lane, Hurlingham Park, London SW6 3DP. Tel: 0171 731 0160.

British Society for Music Therapy – 25 Rosslyn Avenue, East Barnet, Herts EN4 8DH. Tel: 0181 368 8879.

Horticultural Therapy – Goulds Ground, Vallis Way, Frome, Somerset BA11 3DW. Tel/fax: 01373 464782.

Rudolf Steiner Organisation – 35 Park Road, London NW1 6XT. Tel: 0171 723 4400.

RELIGIOUS WORK

Anglican / Church of England

The Advisory Board of Ministry – Church House, Great Smith Street, London SW1P 3NZ. Tel: 0171 222 9011.

The Vocations Adviser – Church Army HQ, Independents Road, Blackheath, London SE3 9LG. Tel: 0181 318 1226.

Baptist Church

Baptist Union of GB – Baptist House, PO Box 44, 129 The Broadway, Didcot, Oxfordshire OX11 8RT. Tel: 01235 512077. (For the Baptist Missionary Society, write to PO Box 49 at this address.)

Church of Scotland

Assistant Secretary – The Department of Education, The Church of Scotland Office, 121 George Street, Edinburgh EH2 4YN. Tel: 0131 225 5722.

Methodist Church

Methodist Church Formation in Ministry – The Secretary, 25 Marylebone Road, London NW1 5JR. Tel: 0171 486 5502.

Roman Catholic Church

National Religious Vocation Centre – 82 Margaret Street, London W1 8LH. Tel: 0171 631 5173.

Salvation Army

International Headquarters – 101 Queen Victoria Street, London EC4P 4EP. Tel: 0171 236 5222.

United Reformed Church

United Reformed Church Ministries – 86 Tavistock Place, London WC1H 9RT. Tel: 0171 916 2020.

Others

Agency for Jewish Education – 735 High Road, London N12 0US. Tel: 0181 343 8989.

Buddhist Society – 58 Eccleston Square, London SW1V 1PH. Tel: 0171 834 5858.

Christians Abroad – 1 Stockwell Green, London SW9 9HP. Tel: 0171 737 7811.

Fellowship of Independent Evangelical Churches – 3 Church Road, Croydon CR0 1SG. Tel: 0181 681 7422.

Hindu Centre – 39 Grafton Terrace, London NW5 4JA. Tel: 0171 485 8200.

Jews' College – 44a Albert Road, Hendon, London NW4 2SJ. Tel: 0181 203 6427.

Sikh Missionary Society – 10 Featherstone Road, Southall, Middlesex UB2 5AA. Tel: 0181 574 1902.

The Congregational Federation – Congregational Centre, 4 Castle Gate, Nottingham NG1 7AS. Tel: 0115 9413 801.

UK Islamic Mission – 202 North Gower Street, London NW1 2LY. Tel: 0171 387 2157.

Community Work and Advice Work is an AGCAS booklet for graduates, available from CSU, Armstrong House, Oxford Road, Manchester M1 7ED. Tel: 0161 236 9816, ext 250/251.

WORK WITH CHARITIES

Charity Recruitment – 40 Rosebery Avenue, London EC1R 4RN. Tel: 0171 833 0770.

Institute of Charity Fundraising Managers – 5th Floor, Market Towers, 1 Nine Elms Lane, London SW8 5NQ. Tel: 0171 627 3436.

National Council for Voluntary Organisations – Regents Wharf, 8 All Saints Street, London N1 9RL. Tel: 0171 713 6161.

The Volunteer Centre UK – Carriage Row, 183 Eversholt Street, London NW1 1BU. Tel: 0171 388 9888.

Directory of Voluntary Agencies, published by the National Council for Voluntary Organisations. The National Council also publishes information briefings on employment opportunities in the voluntary sector: 'Part 1 – Paid Employment' and 'Part 2 – Unpaid Voluntary Work'.

Working in the Voluntary Sector, published by COIC.

How to Work for a Charity and The *Directory of Volunteering and Employment Opportunities* can be obtained from the publisher – Directory of Social Change, 24 Stephenson Way, London NW1 2DP. Tel: 0171 209 5151.